"Maria, your book is a *great read*! It's full to bursting with innovative and invaluable tips for increasing website profits. The chapter *"From Prospects to Purchasers: The Psychological Motivators"* is a *power-packed bomb*—it blew my mind!"

—Mekhola Majumdar, www.writingwealth.com

"I'm so glad you've written a book that teaches exactly how you produce copywriting masterpieces that sell like crazy. One day, I hope to be half as good a web copywriter as you."

—Ardi Bakri, Webmaster, Singapore,
http://www.clubs5678.com

"Web Copy That Sells is an *absolute necessity* for anyone who wants to write riveting web copy. The blueprint alone slashes hours off of writing. Thanks, Maria, for a power-packed book!"

—Nancy Travis, Web Copywriter, Miami, Florida

"I have a pretty thorough grounding in offline copywriting, but I've found the methods and techniques described in your book quite *mind-boggling*. They go beyond common practice and embrace a practicality that makes the whole discipline very comfortable. Much of what you've introduced is applicable to offline work as well. I thank you for *expanding my vision* of how this craft can be practiced and for opening my mind to developing a much broader array of tools to use."

—Bruce Midgett, Owner, MBP Custom Publishers,
Missoula, Montana

"Maria, I just finished the first read-through of your book, *Web Copy That Sells*. Boy, you are some kind of genius or something! I've read tons of copywriting books and as I read through your book, I kinda got a hole in my stomach, but also got really excited realizing how my approach has not been all that well thought out—and how it could be a whole lot better! I've gotten good conversions before your book came around, and I can't even imagine what's going to happen when I implement your ideas! What impresses me is your ability to teach your techniques so clearly. You've really got a gift, Maria."

—Paul Schlegel, St. Louis, Missouri,
www.learnfastearnfast.com

"Maria, I cannot even begin to tell you how much I'm enjoying myself writing copy the way you've taught it in your book! I just love it—and whenever I write copy for anyone, they're always *blown away by the results*! And I've just barely gotten started. I actually look forward to getting out of bed every single day to write this way. I'm so grateful that I found your book! This has *changed my life*—and at a time when I was stagnating after doing non-stop traditional marketing for over 20 years. So glad I found your book—so glad, so glad . . ."
—Susan B. Loebl, Web Copywriting Specialist,
www.webcopywriting.us

"Maria, I shared some of the concepts I learned from your book with the president of one company and a few other close friends—all of whom had a similar *"Aha!" experience* as I did . . . It had nothing to do with me, of course. It was your book—and I told them so . . . What a wonderful paradigm shift—your ideas are definitely profound and mind-blowing."
—Robert Durant, Raleigh, North Carolina

"By the time you finish reading Maria's incredible book, *you'll know more than 99% of your competitors* when it comes to making web visitors pull out their credit cards and buy what you're selling.

"I've invested a ton of money in my copywriting education over the years and there isn't anything like her *easy-to-follow, step-by-step blueprint* for writing irresistible web copy.
—Tony Ostian, Certified Master of Web Copywriting,
www.webCopyGuy.com

"Maria, you have definitely revolutionized the proper techniques for writing web copy that sells! Your book is absolutely the most astonishing, and *easy-to-follow guide* for business owners who want to take their business 10 steps forward and start making a name for themselves in the online world. Thank you, Maria. *You're absolutely amazing!*"
—Carlos Garcia, Publisher, *Wealthy Secrets Newsletter,*
London, Ontario, Canada

Praise for *Web Copy That Sells*

"Maria, I'm very impressed with your book! You're the first one to really make a convincing argument and show concrete evidence why writing for the web (especially e-mail copy) is quite different from writing for the offline markets in several aspects. Thanks for your enlightening material."

—Kevin Wilke, Founder of PureNetProfits.com
and Cofounder of NitroMarketing.com

Web Copy That Sells belongs on the desktop of any e-marketer who wants to make more sales and profits *without spending a nickel* more on advertising. Maria's web copy tips and techniques are like oxygen that'll breathe more life into your websites and e-mail campaigns. Chapter 3 alone is worth 100 times the price you'll pay for this copywriting book."

—Alex Mandossian, Web Traffic Conversion Strategist
and President of www.CopywritingCoach.com

"Without a doubt, Maria Veloso 'wrote the book' on how to turn a website into a selling machine. *Web Copy That Sells* is among the most important marketing books ever written. It should be required reading for all Internet marketers, webmasters and copywriters. Maria has simplified the craft of writing direct-response web copy down to an easy, step-by-step blueprint that is so appealing even my wife has decided to become a copywriter!"

—Tim Russ, Editor, *Candle Light Magazine*

"After spending thousands upon thousands of dollars getting information from almost every Internet and marketing expert out there, I can say that, without a doubt, Maria Veloso's book, *Web Copy That Sells,* is the best investment that anyone wanting a profitable career on the Internet could make."

—Rick Miller, Certified Master of Web Copywriting,
author of "Internet Mind Control,"
Founder of ScientificInternetMarketing.com

"When it comes to writing the words on your website that make people pull out their credit cards and buy whatever you're selling, Maria Veloso is an absolute genius. But what's truly amazing is her singular skill in *simplifying* the craft of writing web copy that sells into a discipline that's both *learnable* and infinitely *easy*."

—Thomas Myer, Freelance Technical Copywriter,
http://www.myerman.com

"Maria, I recently read *Web Copy That Sells,* and I've experienced an incredible side effect as a result of two sentences that leapt out at me from your book. I was running a pay-per-click campaign on Overture, and I was getting dismal click-through rates of 0.5 to 2.0 percent. After I implemented what I learned from your book in my Overture description, my click-through rates skyrocketed to 5.4 to 15.4 percent overnight. In the past, I almost gave up because although I was getting sales, I was paying most of the profit to Overture. Now I get more hits, more conversions, and I'm keeping the profits! Thanks, Maria, for your dynamite pay-per-click phrases."

—Terry Fisher, "The LottoMasta"
www.lottery-and-lotto.com

"I must admit your book, *Web Copy That Sells,* is probably the best book I've read to date about web copywriting—or copywriting, for that matter. Unlike the other books out there, *Web Copy That Sells* actually plugged me into my prospects' thought processes, showing me step-by-step how to sell to them. I'll *never* write copy the same again. Your work will no doubt have a profound impact on my bottom line. . . . Thanks Maria!"

—Scott Krech, Creator of InternetAudioMadeEasy.com

"I am just blown away by the way Maria Veloso takes complicated copywriting techniques, such as applying psychological tactics, and explains them so that I, a copywriting newbie, can easily understand them. And not only understand them conceptually, but understand how to use them and feel comfortable using them in my writing. Maria is nothing short of a *copywriting genius* and *Web Copy That Sells* is the most outstanding book for learning how to sell on the web."

—Tim Warren, Dallas, Texas,
CEO of GreatMarketingStuff.com

"Maria—I just love your book, *Web Copy That Sells*! I spend about $30,000 a year on copywriting education, and I have to say this is the best on web copy—hands down!"

—Lou V., Schererville, Indiana

"Maria, *Web Copy That Sells* is definitely an awesome book—thoroughly researched, practical, and well overdue. I've skimmed through all of the chapters and I've got to say *wow*! This has got to be the first how-to book that's actually a how-to book on copywriting that explains the science behind copy! I'm learning your methods in earnest. I think this is dangerous stuff! Thank you, thank you, and thank you!"

—Jon Relunia, Personal Digital Assistant (PDA) Learning
Coach, www.speeduplearning.com

WEB COPY THAT SELLS

*The Revolutionary Formula
for Creating Killer Copy
Every Time*

Maria Veloso

AMACOM

American Management Association
New York · Atlanta · Brussels · Chicago · Mexico City · San Francisco
Shanghai · Tokyo · Toronto · Washington, D. C.

Special discounts on bulk quantities of AMACOM books are available to corporations, professional associations, and other organizations. For details, contact Special Sales Department, AMACOM, a division of American Management Association, 1601 Broadway, New York, NY 10019.
Tel.: 212-903-8316.   Fax: 212-903-8083
Web site: www.amacombooks.org

This publication is designed to provide accurate and authoritative information in regard to the subject matter covered. It is sold with the understanding that the publisher is not engaged in rendering legal, accounting, or other professional service. If legal advice or other expert assistance is required, the services of a competent professional person should be sought.

Library of Congress Cataloging-in-Publication Data

Veloso, Maria.
   Web copy that sells : the revolutionary formula for creating killer copy every time / Maria Veloso.
     p. cm.
   Includes bibliographical references and index.
   ISBN-10: 0-8144-7249-4
   ISBN-13: 978-0-8144-7249-1
   1. Electronic commerce.   2. Web sites—Design.   3. Internet marketing.   4. Internet advertising.   I. Title.

HF5548.32.V45   2004
658.8′72—dc22

                                    2004015067

Printing number

10   9   8   7   6

With Profound Gratitude
To J.C.
who makes all things possible
and without whom my life would have
neither purpose nor direction.

Contents

Foreword

On July 23, 2000, I received an e-mail with the following subject line:

> SUBJECT: Mark, here are the Top 10 Reasons Why You
> Need to Have Me Working for You

I get hundreds of e-mail a day—but the subject line of the e-mail stopped me dead in my tracks. The e-mail was from a woman named Maria Veloso. Her e-mail began as follows:

> Dear Mark,
> Have you ever wished you could "clone" yourself so that all the ideas you have "in development" can materialize with lightning speed?

Then, the e-mail went on to give 10 compelling reasons why Maria would be an asset to my company, Aesop Marketing Corporation.

I was sufficiently intrigued by her e-mail that I phoned her and told her that I might have a position for which she would qualify. However, I gave her this word of warning:

"It's the most miserable job you could possibly have in my company."

When I told her it was the job of a copywriter, she was puzzled. "Why do you think that's such a miserable job, Mark?" she asked.

"Because you'll be writing copy for me," I said. I told her I'd be extremely difficult to please because I had excruciatingly high standards. I also told her that because I had always done my own copywriting and never trusted anyone to write on my behalf, I'd constantly be cracking the whip on anyone who had the misfortune of becoming my copywriter.

Without skipping a beat, she said, "I'm up to the challenge, Mark."

I shook my head, feeling sorry that this woman didn't know what she was getting herself into. I agreed to interview her soon thereafter. She showed me her copywriting samples, and it was easy to tell that she was skilled in writing copy for the offline markets. But I wondered how well she could learn how to write web copy.

That's when she told me she's been a big fan of my unique approach to online copywriting for years—and that she had bought several products and services from my company over the years on the strength of the copy I wrote. She was eager to learn my style of copywriting, and reiterated that she wanted to become my copywriting clone.

"Okay," I said. "You're hired!"

At the time, my company (Aesop) was already a multimillion-dollar enterprise, and was enjoying international fame in Internet marketing circles because of the unconventional, nonconformist marketing campaigns we were running.

When I gave Maria her first copywriting assignment, I could tell she was eager to prove her skill as a copywriter. Three days later, when she handed me the copy she wrote, I told her flat out that it wasn't the way I wanted copy at Aesop to be written. She definitely had great copywriting skills, but they were tailored for the offline world—not the web.

I thought my rebuff would discourage her, but she was undaunted. She was determined to learn the right way of writing web copy. Thus began my mentorship of Maria Veloso. I began to teach her the little-known mechanics and art of writing for the Internet buying public. She took copious notes, and was a quick study. In as little as a few weeks' time, I began to see her web copywriting begin to show promise.

In October 2000, two months after she started working for me, she handed me a six-page copy piece that pulled in *$18,000 in two days*. That was when I was convinced she was a *killer copywriter*. But that wasn't the end of her copywriting education. Not by a long shot.

Over the following months and years, I continued to conduct the most ambitious (and expensive) market testing ever attempted in Internet marketing. I hired an entire staff of programmers, statisticians, and analysts, whose only job was to test every conceivable element of the copy we produced at Aesop—from headlines to price points, offers, guarantees, formats, involvement devices, e-mail subject lines, lead-ins, etc. You name it—I had my research staff test it, take the raw data, and convert it into usable form.

People called me "The Fanatic of Online Market Testing" but I rather enjoyed having that reputation. It was all my attempt to identify those seemingly marginal elements of web copy and online marketing communications that made a significant difference in our sales figures. Because Aesop had amassed a database of millions of names, consisting of customers, subscribers, and prospects, we had the luxury of conducting huge marketing tests, wherein our test samples were as large as 20,000 names apiece—a number that was larger than most other companies' entire mailing lists. As a result, we produced the most scientifically validated—and conclusive—results ever obtained.

For 15 months, Maria had a ringside seat and witnessed the blow-by-blow action being churned out by my marketing statisticians and analysts. She was privy to some of the most priceless pieces of marketing intelligence ever assembled.

She saw, for instance that many of the concepts that I had introduced to Internet marketing, such as the *Zeigarnik effect, cognitive dissonance,* the *linear path,* and so on (see Chapter 3), had a dramatic effect on click-through rates and sales conversions. She saw the full-scale findings of what has become known as my *Confidential Internet Intelligence Manuscript* that my marketing staff had assembled at a cost of over $237,000—a manuscript that revealed *e-mail marketing strategies* that work (see Chapter 5), among other things.

Having had the benefit of all this, Maria's copywriting had nowhere to go but up. Being armed with as much web copywriting ammunition as any of the copywriting greats alive, she took the ball and ran with it. She's one of the very few copywriters in the world who "get" web copywriting. I am deeply gratified to have been instrumental in her becoming one of the top copywriting professionals in the industry today.

That said, it is also flattering to see that Maria has taken many of the concepts I pioneered and tested, and distilled them into the book you now have in your hands. If you're tempted to take the concepts she presents on these pages for granted, I'm here to tell you that you're walking past a gold mine. If the results of my extensive marketing research are any indication, I can say, without a doubt, that the information in this book is well-founded and accurate.

Some of the information in this book is indescribably powerful. I encourage you to use it ethically to take your online sales—or your copywriting career if you're a copywriter—to the highest level.

Mark Joyner
#1 Best-Selling Author of
MindControlMarketing.com
and others
Auckland, New Zealand
March 2004

Acknowledgment

This book would not have been possible if it weren't for the valuable lessons I learned from my mentor and friend, Mark Joyner. I owe a debt of gratitude to him for more things than I could possibly sum up here.

Mark was the first person I had ever seen use the editorial style of direct-response copywriting online. His approach to copywriting, where he wrapped his sales pitch in the cushions of an editorial piece, has become the copywriting model that I employ exclusively. It was Mark who taught me that writing sales copy for the web is distinctly different from writing sales copy for the offline (brick-and-mortar) world. Mark also taught me the significance of the prospect's frame of mind when it comes to selling (and it became the basis of my book, *Frame-of-Mind Marketing: How to Convert Your Online Prospects into Customers*). Mark also introduced me to many of the psychological devices that I use in writing web copy, which have produced the signature model of web copywriting with which I'm identified today.

▶ *The Zeigarnik effect.* Although this principle has become widely used among marketers in recent years, Mark was the pioneer at successfully applying it to web copy and Internet marketing—along with the "linear path" methodology, which is part of his "Source of the Nile" theory.

▶ *Cognitive dissonance.* To my knowledge, this concept had never been mentioned in a marketing book prior to Mark's inclusion of it in his marketing course titled *1001 Killer Internet Marketing Tactics.* Although other marketers may have previously used the cognitive dissonance technique, as well as the Zeigarnik effect, no one has ever identified the tandem concepts in relation to business and marketing or established their scientific validity the way Mark has.

Finally, the bulk of the e-mail strategies I discuss in Chapter 4 are owed in no small part to the research spearheaded by Mark at Aesop. For these reasons and more, I consider him the honorary coauthor of this book.

My goal is to bring what I've learned to you.

Maria Veloso
April 2004

Introduction

I cannot teach anybody anything,
I can only make them think.
—Socrates

It never fails. When people ask me what I do for a living, and I say, "I write web copy," I'm met with blank stares. Web copy is such a new term even those who have an Internet presence hardly recognize it. I quickly explain, "Web copy simply means the words that make visitors to your website pull out their credit cards and buy your product or service."

Invariably, I get an enthusiastic response. People tell me about their plans to sell this product or that service on the Internet, but they simply don't know how to do it. Others tell me they already have a website, but it's not doing a good job selling.

I've sold everything from books to hair restoration products, self-improvement programs, membership clubs, tax-saving programs, seminars, and more on the web, and in the process I've learned how to take a casual website visitor and turn that surfer into a prospect and, subsequently, into a customer—all through the sheer power of words.

It's simply amazing. Never before has there ever been such a great demand for a service. It seems as though just about everyone needs web copy written, and they usually need it "right now."

Words are the true currency of the web. While it may seem counterintuitive, it's no wonder that the single most important ingredient in a commercial website is *web copy*. Words make the sale.

Picture a website with cutting-edge design, cool graphics, interactive bells and whistles, and sophisticated e-commerce infrastructure. Compare that with a stark website with no graphics or cool technology—just web copy on a plain white background. Which of the two websites is more likely to sell a product or service?

Most people are surprised to learn that it is the one with the words. Because selling on the web is text-driven, nothing happens until someone writes the words that get people to click, sign up, read, register, order, subscribe, or buy whatever you're selling. According to a four-year study, conducted by Stanford University and the Poynter Institute and published in 2000, of the habits of Internet news readers on normally scrolling screens, "the first thing people look at on a webpage tends to be text."

For this reason, if you have a website (or plan to create one) that sells a product or service, you need to hire a web copywriter—someone who understands how to write web copy that sells—or learn the craft of web copywriting yourself, which brings me to the reason I decided to write this book. Every time I surf the Internet, I come across countless websites that are so poorly written, I can't imagine them generating a single sale. I come across websites with excellent products and services, but with weak web copy that doesn't do the products and services justice. It's a shame, because the web provides the most incredible channel for marketing virtually anything to anybody in any part of the world.

Adding to the difficulty for the small entrepreneur or the opportunity for newcomers to web writing is the fact that there is a scarcity of web copywriting specialists equipped to take on the unique challenge of web communication and online selling. This situation is unlikely to change in the foreseeable future, even with the increasing numbers of professional writers transitioning into web copywriting. As a result, even if you're a website owner or Internet entrepreneur who could find and afford good web copywriters, chances are, the good ones would be too busy to take on your project.

My solution—and my reason for writing this book—is to teach you the principles of web copywriting so you can write web copy yourself. Whether you are a businessperson writing your own copy or a writer entering the business or transitioning from other kinds advertising copywriting, my goal is to teach you how to take your writing skills and apply them to web writing. Web copy that converts prospects into customers is a discipline all its own. It's a highly specialized genre of writing that combines marketing wherewithal with a deep understanding of the Internet's unique culture, mind-set, psychology, and language.

What most online businesspeople and some professional copywriters don't realize is that web copywriting is distinctly different from any other kind of advertising copy and offline marketing communications. It is also quite different from writing content for the web. Of course, it also bears some similarities to all of these.

Selling on the web is text-driven. Nothing happens until someone writes the words that get people to respond. In this, it is similar to other types of direct-response copywriting; therefore, to write good web copy you must first understand the fundamental principles of direct-response copywriting. Throughout *Web Copy That Sells,* you will find generally accepted rules and conventions of offline copywriting, as well as direct-response copywriting principles that run parallel to those used in web copywriting. As you progress through the chapters, you will begin to see the remarkable (as well as the subtle) differences between direct-response selling online and offline.

On the other hand, one of the biggest mistakes online businesses and advertising professionals make is to take marketing principles that work well in the offline world and try to force them to work on the web. Many principles that are effective in direct mail, print ads, radio ads, and infomercials simply do not translate well on the web. In fact, they can even kill sales.

Who needs this book? You do, if you are

▶ An Internet marketer, entrepreneur, or website owner who sells (or plans to sell) a product or service online via your own direct response website

▶ A professional who approves, plans, and executes Internet marketing campaigns (marketing or advertising vice presidents, managers, and directors and MIS managers)

▶ A writer (or copywriter) who is tired of being underpaid and barely earning a living—and who wants to transition to the lucrative specialty of web copywriting

► A webmaster who wants to learn the skill of web copy-writing in order to expand the services you provide your clients

► Someone with moderate-to-good writing skills who wants to become a highly paid professional writer in one of the hottest, most in-demand fields in today's marketplace

Whether or not you aspire to become a professional web copywriter, you can take the principles presented in this book and apply them to any website, incorporate them into your marketing communications (e-mail, online advertising, newsletters, etc.), and generate measurably increased sales and profits.

There are various ways to market on the web, not the least of which are branding and institutional advertising, but I've written this book specifically for websites that depend on direct-response web copy to induce sales-advancing action from a single exposure. However, even if your goal is to write another type of web copy, you will benefit from the principles revealed in this book because they will sharpen the edges of your marketing messages, making them more effective.

I specialize in *direct-response web copy* because I like the accountability this field demands. It must produce *immediate* and *measurable* results. Therefore, it is ultimately a more rewarding and gratifying endeavor for me. I've been writing advertising copy since 1977 and specializing in web copywriting since 1996, which gives me a broader perspective of the craft than most people have. Yet I "stand on the shoulders of giants," learning from those who came before me—masters of influence like Robert Cialdini and marketing legends like

Rosser Reeves, Victor Schwab, Robert Collier, and Eugene Schwartz—whose powerful concepts I've battle-tested and fine-tuned for the web.

WHAT THIS BOOK WILL DO FOR YOU ▼

When I encountered the World Wide Web in 1996, I had 19 years of copywriting experience under my belt, but I soon discovered that writing copy for the web was a highly specialized craft. There was a multitude of things to learn—and unlearn. It's my goal to teach you the things I've learned and help you avoid some of the errors I made.

As you go through the book, here are some of the tools you'll find:

▶ The most powerful psychological principles underlying web copy that sells are explored in Chapter 3, which offers devices, strategies, tactics, and tips that can make any website sizzle with sales activity.

▶ The formula for measuring the selling quotient of your copy (Chapter 4) shows you how to evaluate your copy's selling ability and how to get an immediate boost in your response rate.

▶ In Chapter 5 you'll discover the amazing power of e-mail marketing and how to write attention-grabbing e-mail copy.

▶ In Chapter 6, I show you how to write compelling online ads, newsletters (or e-zines), autoresponder messages, and other marketing communications that can propel your online business to uncharted heights.

► After you've learned the craft of web copywriting, Chapter 7 reveals the four-step foolproof secret to success in all your copywriting endeavors.

On the web, you simply can't model successful websites and expect to succeed. You need to model the *process* through which the success was attained, *not* the outcome of that process. For that reason, we examine the steps, the psychology, and the philosophies that are considered in writing successful web copy rather than modeling the web copy itself and trying to adapt it where it isn't appropriate. Instead of simply presenting formulas or power words and phrases, I'll demonstrate how to acquire the *mind-set* with which to view websites, e-mail, and all other marketing communications so that you, too, can write web copy that sells. Among other things, you'll find an exercise that will help you become a great web copywriter in five hours or less and a unique copywriting approach based on five simple questions, which, when answered, make the web copy practically write itself.

Very few people truly understand the complexities of communicating in the relatively new medium called the Internet. However, by the time you finish reading this book, you'll know more about web copywriting than 99 percent of the population. More important, you will be able to parlay that specialized knowledge into a six-figure income in the field of web copywriting or dramatically increase the sales of your website.

1

Getting Started:
The Dynamics of Web Selling

"Don't worry that you'll take a shot and you'll miss.
The fact is, you'll miss every shot you don't take."
—Anonymous

In the advertising world, the words employed to communicate a sales message in an advertisement or commercial are called *advertising copy,* and the people who write these words are known as *copywriters.* (This term should not be confused with *copyright,* which is a legal mechanism that protects your ownership of what you write.)

Similarly, *web copy* refers to the words employed to communicate a sales message on the web, and the people who write these words are *web copywriters.* Although distinctly different in tone from advertising copy, web copy has the same objectives; that is, to generate leads, customers, sales, and, consequently, profits for a website. (Web copy should not be confused with web content, which consists of words written for the web for the purpose of informing, communicating, entertaining, or edifying the reader, not necessarily communicating a sales or marketing message.)

Web copywriting is one of the most exciting crafts and professions I know of. I often equate it with alchemy, but whereas alchemy is the science that turns base metals into gold, web copywriting turns words into money seemingly out of thin air. Think about it. The Internet is the only place where anyone can truly market every day for little or no money and have the chance at making a fortune. Personally, I have seen many people do it—even on a shoestring budget.

Whatever your writing skills are, don't worry! Practically anyone with moderate-to-good writing skills can learn how to write web copy. One of the best copywriters in the offline world, Joe Sugarman, almost flunked English in high school. One of his copywriting students, a grapefruit farmer who had never written sales copy, made millions of dollars over the years using sales copy he wrote to sell grapefruit by mail.

THREE FUNDAMENTAL RULES FOR WRITING WEB COPY THAT SELLS ▼

It amuses me that whenever I run a successful campaign with great web copy, I find a few dozen copycats mimicking certain parts of my work. I chuckle because invariably they have copied the words but failed to duplicate the *strategy* or *tactic* behind the words, which is what really makes the copy effective. What is my writing strategy? In some ways it boils down to three relatively simple, but not so obvious, rules.

Rule 1. Don't Make Your Website Look Like an Ad

Depending on which source you believe, the average person is exposed to anywhere between 1,500 (*Media Literacy Report* published by Unicef) and 5,000 (Charles Pappas, Yahoo! *Internet Life* columnist) advertising messages per day from TV, billboards, radio, the Internet, practically everywhere we turn. The last thing we want to see when we land on a website is yet another ad.

Yet many online businesses seem to go out of their way to make their websites look like ads, billboards, or other commercial media. Don't fall into this trap and turn away potential customers. Your website should provide the solid information that your prospect is looking for, and it should have an editorial feel to it. Above all, it should be free of hype. Why? Because people usually go online to find information. Few people log on saying, "I can't wait to see ads, and I can't wait to buy stuff!" No, that usually doesn't happen.

People go online to find information. That's why they call it the information superhighway. Even if they are shopping for something—say a DVD player or a hair restoration product—they are generally seeking information, not advertising, about those products. There is a myth that the Internet is an advertising medium or one big shopping channel. It's *not*.

Here's the first distinction between offline advertising copy and effective web copy. Web copy needs to have an editorial feel to it; that is, it *cannot* look or feel like a sales pitch.

Editorial-Style Web Headlines

▶ Don't Buy a DVD Player Unless It Meets These 5 Criteria

▶ 9 Facts You Must Know Before You Buy Any Product That Promises to Grow Hair or Stop Hair Loss

▶ Can Streaming Audio Really Double Your Website Sales? A recent Internet research study says you *can*. [Courtesy of InternetAudioMadeEasy.com.]

Where does the selling come in? It comes from *compelling content—expertly crafted for hidden selling.* In plain English, this means: Develop irresistible content that slides smoothly into a covert sales pitch for your product.

Why? Because people online do not want to be sold to. A study conducted by web usability experts John Morkes and Jakob Nielsen (reported in a paper titled *Concise, Scannable and Objective: How to Write for the Web*) showed that web users "detest anything that seems like marketing fluff or overly hyped language ('marketese') and prefer factual information." If web visitors ever do get sold on something, they want to be finessed, not bombarded by blatant advertising.

It bears repeating that your sales pitch should not sound like an ad, but rather it should read like an editorial, testimonial, advice, case study, or endorsement. If you want an example of this kind of writing in the brick-and-mortar (meaning *offline*) world, think "advertorial" (editorial-style ads) or press release.

In the offline world, editorial-style ads boost readership significantly over standard-looking ads. David Ogilvy, legendary advertising man, wrote in his book, *Ogilvy on Advertising*, "There is no law which says that advertisements have to look like advertisements. If you make them look like editorial pages, you will attract more readers. Roughly *six times as many people read the average article as the average advertisement* [emphasis mine]. Very few advertisements are read by more than one reader in twenty." In fact, in a split-run test conducted in *Reader's Digest*, an editorial-style ad boosted response by 80 percent over the standard ad layout.

When I worked as the director of creative web writing at Aesop, Mark Joyner commissioned extensive in-house marketing research to test the effectiveness of every imaginable element of our web copy and other online marketing communications. To give you an idea of the magnitude of the research, Aesop's database consisted of millions of Internet entrepreneurs, and we frequently tested copy elements on samples of 20,000 names for each testing variable. The sales results I witnessed at Aesop made clear to me the effectiveness of the editorial style of copywriting. In the tests in which I've been involved, editorial-style web copy outpulls sales letter–style Web copy every single time. Remember, people generally tune out ads, but they tune in to editorial information. (See Figure 1.1.)

Rule 2. Stop Readers Dead in Their Tracks

Online business owners spend a lot of time and money trying to get traffic to their websites. Building web traffic is very important, but it won't mean a thing unless you do one thing

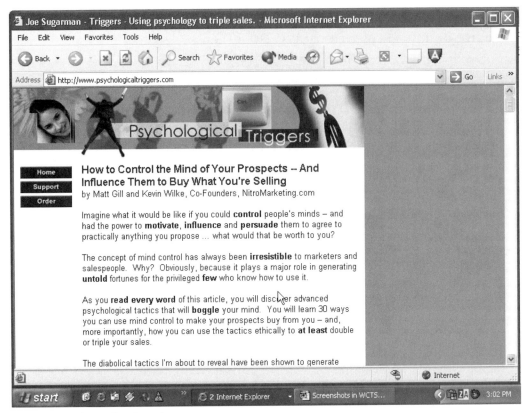

Figure 1.1 Editorial-style web copy.

first. That is, create compelling web copy that will stop them dead in their tracks and get them to do what you want them to do when they get there.

According to Google, as of April 2004, there were about 36 million websites clamoring for attention, not to mention more than 4.28 billion pages of content! It's no wonder, then, that in order for words to wield their magical power on the web, they have to be tailored specifically for the information-flooded Internet public where attention span is a rare commodity.

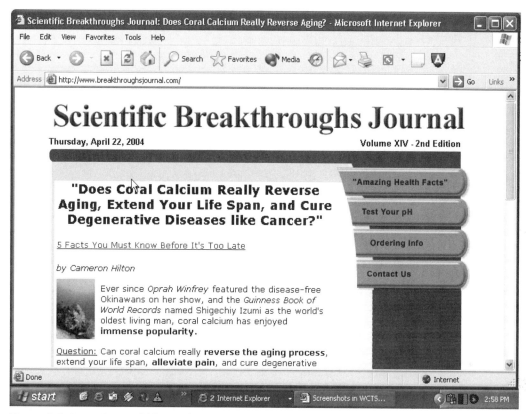

Figure 1.2 Attention-grabbing website.

Fact: If your website is little more than an online brochure for your business, then your website is a very weak selling tool. (See Figure 1.2.)

"Breakthroughs Journal" is a good example of a website that stops visitors dead in their tracks. The headline incites curiosity ("Does Coral Calcium Really Reverse Aging, Extend Your Life Span, and Cure Degenerative Diseases Like Cancer?"), and the subheadline (5 Facts You Must Know Before It's Too Late) injects emotion, drama, and a sense of urgency. Its copy, written in the editorial style, follows through by giving readers a sense that they're reading a news item, not an advertisement.

Rule 3. Capture E-Mail Addresses

For a website to succeed, it must have effective direct-response web copy that induces action from a single exposure. Just think. What's the point in getting someone to come to your website if the site visit doesn't generate a response such as picking up the phone and calling your business, subscribing to your newsletter, signing up for your mailing list, or buying your product or service?

Generating a response means more than impressing web visitors with cool graphics or technology or getting them to bookmark your site. Bookmark lists have become information closets that contain a jumble of sites people never return to, according to William Jones, a research associate professor at the Information School at the University of Washington (Lisa Guernsey, "Now Where Was I? New Ways to Revisit Web Sites," *New York Times,* January 22, 2004). Jones noted that "Only hyperorganized users sort sites into folders, clean out dead links or click on inscrutable addresses to figure out why they were bookmarked in the first place." I've heard a ballpark estimate that fewer than one percent of Internet users actually return to sites they've bookmarked. What good can that possibly do you?

What's the point in having cutting-edge web design, eye-popping graphics, and a sophisticated e-commerce infrastructure if you are unable to entice your visitors long enough for them to do what you want them to do?

If you are selling something on your website, chances are that less than 5 percent of your site's visitors will ever buy your product. Conversion rates vary with each industry, but the typical healthy rate for online stores is 0.5 percent (.005) to 1.5 percent (.015), according to the *Bock Newsletter* on Yahoo! Store (issue 32). "Conversion rates of 2 percent to 5 percent are fairly typical today," according to a report titled *Getting Clicks with Casual Customers* at CNETNews.com. Even the best marketers with the most successful websites seldom convert more than 5 percent of their web visitors into customers.

What happens to the 95 percent of your web visitors who came and went? For most websites, nothing. Those prospects are gone for good, never to return. That's why it is absolutely essential for your website to have an opt-in mechanism. The odds are low that people will buy from you the first time they visit your website. After all, they don't even know you. Rather than lose them, ask for something that is easier and less intimidating than pulling out a credit card—ask them to give you their e-mail address. It's a simple, nonthreatening way to initiate a relationship.

Trust, as we all know, is an important issue in e-commerce, and finding ways to build trust in an online environment is a continuing challenge for Internet businesses. On the web, people buy from people they *like* and *trust*. They like people who provide them with information they need, who are not overly aggressive in trying to market their products, and who are easy to do business with. They trust people who deliver on the promises they make, who take time to develop a relationship with them, who provide good customer service, and who have an articulated privacy policy to which they strictly adhere. Capturing contact information is the first step in developing rapport

"How to Pay Less for Almost Everything"
The world's best *bargain hunters* and haggle hounds reveal their **secrets** for easily finding the *lowest prices* on things you buy everyday. Once you learn these simple, but **ingenious** strategies for getting more and spending less, it's like having given yourself a **20% (or more) pay raise** -- tax-free!

Send for this **FREE report** today. Simply fill in your name and address in the form below -- and this **valuable** report will be sent to your e-mail box automatically *within minutes*!

[Your contact information will be handled with the *strictest confidence*, and will never be sold or shared with third parties.]

☐	**Send me my FREE report now.**
Email address:	
First Name:	
Last Name:	

Add Address

Figure 1.3 Exit pop-up opt-in offer.

with prospective customers and in building a relationship that will foster online sales—now and in the future. (See Figure 1.3.)

An opt-in offer, such as "How to Pay Less . . ." is one way to capture a visitor's e-mail address. (See Chapter 2 for a complete discussion of opt-in mechanisms.)

THE FIRST LOOK

▼

What is the most important element of a website? The first screen (or the first eyeful) is the prime selling space of your website, and what you put in it makes or breaks its success. Do not confuse the first screen with the first *page*, which is often referred to as the *home page* or the *landing page* of a website. The first screen is *only* the part of the page that appears on the screen when you land on a website; it's the screen you see before your scroll down or sideways. In a print newspaper, its counterpart is the information above the fold, which draws maximum readership.

Often, the first screen is the first, last, and only thing people see on a website before they click away. For this reason, *don't* make the mistake many companies do of putting a large logo or your company name in gigantic letters on that screen. Some companies do this for branding purposes, but in most cases the company name and logo don't have to take up half of the first screen. Your logo doesn't need to be large—it's not a selling feature. While it may stroke your ego, it won't increase your sales. An oversized logo wastes valuable selling space.

Conversely, a headline *must* be included in the first screen. It is the most important component of a webpage. Consider how pointless it would be for a newspaper to have no headline. A website without a headline is just as pointless, yet it's remarkable how many websites fail to put a headline in this prime selling space.

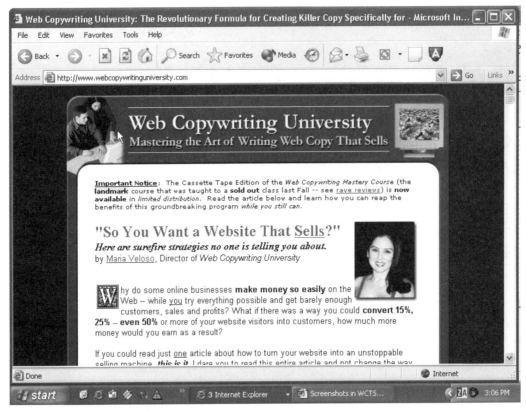

Figure 1.4 Targeted headline captures attention.

In my years of surfing the web, I've observed that the majority of commercial websites that do have headlines have weak, uninteresting headlines, and, as a result, they are missing a critical opportunity to attract and retain website visitors. (See Figure 1.4.)

On my Web Copywriting University website, I used the headline, "So You Want a Website That Sells?" followed by the subheadline, "Here are surefire strategies no one is telling you about." This headline calls out to a target audience: those who want a website that sells. A headline that calls out to a *specific* target audience is one way to capture the attention of the web visitor. Contrariwise, when you call out to everyone, you often call out to no one.

I started the body copy with the following question: "Why do some online businesses make money so easily on the web—while you try everything possible and get barely enough customers, sales and profits?" I do this because when you ask a question, the brain is compelled to answer it. Readers are more likely to believe an idea that their brain seems to have come up with on its own than an idea that is presented from outside.

Never underestimate the power of your reader's imagination. Compare the impact of the following two examples (one a question and one a statement):

1. What if there were a way you could convert 15 percent, 25 percent—even 50 percent or more—of your website visitors into customers, how much more money would you earn as a result?

2. Your business can convert 15 percent, 25 percent—even 50 percent or more—of your website visitors into customers and earn a lot of money.

Notice that the statement makes a claim that a reader may or may not believe. Contrast that with the question, which introduces the *possibility* of an ideal scenario and allows the brain to draw its own conclusions and paint its own pictures.

I like to use "What if . . ." questions or "Imagine what would happen if . . ." or "Think back . . ." That way, you let your readers envision the scene for themselves. Robert Collier, publisher and author of several books, most notable of which is the *Robert Collier Letter Book*, which many consider the bible for writing sales letters, said, "The reader colors that mental picture with his own imagination, which is more potent than all the brushes of all the world's artists." The things that people imagine about your product or service often exceed reality.

Notice that I featured a powerful testimonial very early on the web copy. Why? This puts a blanket of credibility on the rest of the copy. Therefore, everything the visitor reads from that point on is influenced by that glowing testimonial, which makes it more believable.

WEB COPY DOs AND DON'Ts ▼

Do strive to write in a conversational style—one person talking to another person. The more friendly and approachable, the better.

Do use contractions. When people talk, they use many contractions. Using contractions helps you sound like you are just one person talking to another. It's intimate, and it increases readership. Use "I've" instead of "I have," "it's" instead of "it is," "we'll" instead of "we will."

Do use common colloquialisms. A colloquialism is an informal, often entertaining word or phrase used in everyday conversation. When you use colloquialisms, you draw your reader closer because you appear more familiar, more friendly, more up close and personal instead of distant and at arm's length.

Use colloquialisms that are understandable to most people with a reasonable familiarity with the English language. Some colloquialisms that have found their way to mainstream online communications include:

dough	money
laid-back	calm and relaxed
make waves	cause trouble
bent out of shape	become upset
come up for air	take a break
cool	great
defect	glitch
twenty grand	$20,000
keep your cool	remain calm
blown away	greatly impressed
megabucks	a lot of money
blow a fuse	lose your temper
bummed	depressed
con	deceive
has deep pockets	has a good source of money
glitzy	fashionable
honcho	boss
get a kick out of	enjoy

Avoid using colloquialisms that may cause misunderstandings. Because the Internet is international, some colloquialisms such as "table a proposal" (postpone the discussion) or "the presentation bombed" (the presentation was a complete failure), which are generally understood by Americans, may mean something that's nearly the opposite to non-Americans.

Don't use corporatespeak. Corporatespeak is jargon commonly used in the business world that often communicates very little to anyone outside a particular industry. I call it *corporate babble* that businesspeople use to sound important.

Consider the following two examples written for a fictitious online business called My Web Store:

1. My Web Store is an e-commerce solutions provider committed to helping people leverage the power of technology to create value-added, win-win cyberspaces that impact global retail markets.

2. My Web Store is a first-of-its-kind form of e-commerce that enables anyone to open a 24/7 online store in as little as 5 minutes—for just $1 a day.

Which statement are web visitors more likely understand? The second, of course. The first employs highfalutin corporate-speak instead of clear, straightforward words and phrases that people can understand. Even if you read it several times, you'd still be wondering what it's trying to say. Corporatespeak such as this is a blatant failure to communicate effectively. Contrast that with example 2, which immediately communicates a clear benefit, singularity, ease, and economy—everything a prospective customer wants to know.

In direct-response marketing, lack of communication is death. If no one understands what you're saying, no one will buy what you're selling. Therefore, avoid corporatespeak and opt for clear, uncomplicated language.

Do use strategically placed testimonials. Testimonials are a powerful sales tool, whether you're selling online or offline. To apply testimonials successfully when selling online, they need to be positioned strategically throughout the website. An ideal place to position a powerful testimonial is very early on in the webpage, preferably in the first or second screen. In that posi-

Figure 1.5 Powerful testimonial from PC Magazine *in the first screen.*

tion, the testimonial puts a blanket of credibility on the rest of the copy. (See Figure 1.5.)

HowStuffWorks.com, one of the most frequently visited sites on the web, uses dynamically generated testimonials on its website header, actually displaying a different testimonial every few seconds.

It's also important to sprinkle testimonials strategically throughout your web copy, particularly in areas where they will reinforce your selling arguments. Testimonials are also particularly useful in your order form, right before you ask for the order (*before* your call to action), and in your order confirmation e-mail (to reinforce the sale).

Don't try to impress your readers with your fancy vocabulary. Effective copywriting isn't about making grandiose, highfalutin claims. It is about communicating in a way that people can easily understand.

Don't be pompous (self-important or arrogant). Let the testimonials make you look good. People online don't like marketese or bragging, boastful language.

READING ON THE WEB
▼

How do people read on the web? According to Jakob Nielsen, author of *Homepage Usability: 50 Websites Deconstructed* and holder of 71 patents relating to making the Internet easier to use, "They don't."

Yes, you read that correctly. People *don't* read online. They scan.

Nielsen, together with John Morkes, director of the Human-Computer Interaction Group at Trilogy Software and, like Nielsen, a usability expert, conducted several scientific studies about reading and writing on the web. They discovered that people read web pages very differently than printed pages. The majority (79 percent) skim web pages quickly (stopping only when something interesting catches their eye); only 16 percent read everything word for word. This corroborates the tests conducted by the Poynter Institute for Media Studies, which, using eye-tracking equipment, found that most readers are indeed scanners.

This is very important to those of us who write web copy or sell on the web. It means that writing successful web copy means writing scannable web copy.

Five Ways to Write Scannable Copy

1. Use bulleted lists to summarize content.

2. Highlight (by using **bold** or *italic* fonts or by <u>underlining</u>) selected keywords to help scanners move through your web copy.

3. Write meaningful subheads (as opposed to amusing or clever ones).

4. Present one idea per paragraph.

5. Use the inverted pyramid style of writing; that is, present key points and conclusions first, followed by less important information and background material.

Exercise: Using your scroll bar, scan through a website. Is the copy inviting to read? Does it incorporate elements that make it scannable and engaging—or does it have huge blocks of text that discourage you from reading further? How many times does something in your copy catch your eye and cause you to read something of interest? Make your copy more scannable by applying the five suggested techniques.

Bonus idea: Use boxes to feature interesting anecdotes, stories, testimonials, case histories, and to further break up your web copy into readable, bite-size chunks.

Think about how you read a sales letter that comes in the mail. It's three-dimensional, and it exists in a spatial realm, whereas a webpage is two-dimensional—it's in a flat realm. Whether you realize it or not, you write in a manner suitable for the printed page, not the web, because that's the medium you are accustomed to. There are big differences.

Imagine you have a multiple-page sales letter in your hands. You can view an entire page in one glance, you can shuffle through or skim through the pages quickly, you can go straight to the order form or the last page to read the P.S. (That's why the P.S. is the second-most-read part of a sales letter, because people can get to it in a second.) Now look at a webpage—you see only one screen, which is just a fraction of a page, at a time. You don't have the luxury of shuffling through the pages. The best you can do is use the scroll bar or a mouse click to go from page to page.

Do you see why you can't simply take offline copywriting principles and apply them to the web?

WORDS TELL, EMOTION SELLS ▼

People's emotions are the primary motivating factors for buying. People buy on emotion and justify their purchase with logic. Both on and off the web, a strong copy platform is built on proven emotional drivers such as anger, exclusivity, fear, greed, guilt, and salvation, to name a few.

Take a look at the first screen of the 24 Techniques for Closing the Sale website (Figure 1.6). Notice that good web copy starts with a *dramatic promise.*

Headline: These Ain't Your Granddaddy's Closing Techniques, Boy!

Subheadline: These are 24 of the most **ruthless** tactics—
kept under wraps for years—that can turn even your most
hard-nosed prospects into cash-generating **customers.**

The purpose of the headline—and to a certain extent the subheadline—is to offer compelling information, solve a problem,
take away pain, help someone achieve a goal and fulfill a desire.
Conversational language that sounds the way people do helps
crank up the *emotional volume.*

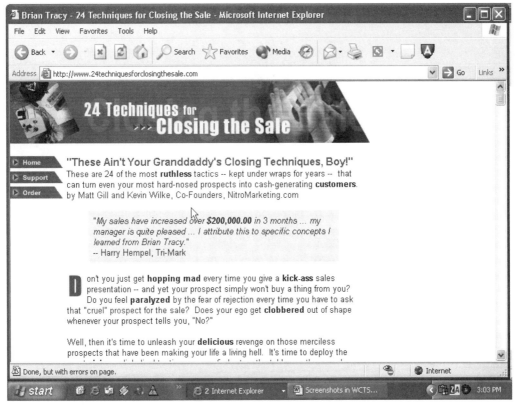

*Figure 1.6 Screenshot of the "24 Techniques for Closing the Sale" website
(www.24TechniquesForClosingTheSale.com).*

The language used on this website carries the emotional intensity of the headline through to its opening paragraph:

> Don't you just get **hopping mad** every time you give a **kick-ass** sales presentation—and yet your prospect simply won't buy a thing from you? Do you feel **paralyzed** by the fear of rejection every time you have to ask that "cruel" prospect for the sale? Does your ego get **clobbered** out of shape whenever your prospect tells you, "No?"

The copy leads the target audience (salespeople) through the excruciating agony of the traditional sales process, a process with which they are all too familiar. It builds the selling proposition on the reader's emotions so that the reader feels the pain and begins to beg for the benefits promised in the headline and subheadline.

Consider the following headlines that I recently found on websites:

Interest Rates Are At Their Lowest in Years
Get Your Home Loan While You Can Still Pre-Qualify
for a More Expensive House or Condo Than You
Can Afford When the Interest Rates Go Up

How to Stop Your Divorce
Even When Your Spouse Wants Out of Your Marriage

**What Will You Do When Creditors Try to Seize Your
Assets to Collect on Debts You Owe Them?**
Is Your Personal Property at Risk?

All three appeal to the reader's fear of loss—one of the greatest motivators. The fact is, people generally go to greater lengths to keep from losing what they have than to gain something of the same (or greater) value. The old sales adage, "Fear of loss is greater than the desire for gain," is as true online as it is in offline selling situations.

HOW TO BECOME A GREAT WEB COPYWRITER IN FIVE HOURS OR LESS ▼

Perhaps you've heard of the concept of modeling success. If you want to achieve success at anything, the fastest way to do it is by modeling the strategies of those who are already successful at it. That way, you take something complex and synthesize it into its essence so you can use it immediately.

You've probably heard of real estate agents going into selling mode by constantly repeating to themselves, "I'm going to sell this house." Annette Bening did this so well in her portrayal of a Realtor in the movie, *American Beauty*. Successful real estate agents start off with the mind-set that the sale is already made. Model the strategy that successful people use to be successful.

In web copywriting, the best way to model success is to select a website that you admire greatly and that you know has produced tons of sales for its owner. Start copying it by hand. *Write the entire sales letter out in your own handwriting.* Write it out two or three times over the next week. Depending on how fast you write, this will take roughly five hours—less if you write quickly or if the sales letter you choose is short. An example of successful web copy that you can handwrite can be found at www.MagicWordsThatMakeYouRich.com.

This takes a lot of discipline, not to mention time, but I assure you, it will be worth the effort. You will not know the value of this until you do it. It's positively eye-opening. I learned this technique from Ted Nicholas, a renowned direct marketer, copywriter, and author of several books.

Once you write this sales letter over and over again, you will start internalizing the wording, the phraseology, the rhythm, even the mind-set of the person who wrote the copy. Your brain assimilates it and you practically step into the mind of the person who wrote it. This is by far the best modeling exercise I've found for accelerating web copywriting skills.

Next time you sit down to write web copy, the wording, the phrasing, and even part of the writer's thought process will have become a part of you, and you will find that it becomes much easier to sit down and begin flowing right into a winning sales piece.

2

A Simple Blueprint for Writing Killer Web Copy

Internalize the Golden Rule of sales that says, "All things being equal, people will do business with, and refer business to, those people they know, like, and trust."
—Bob Burg

Before you write one word of copy, you must first

- ▶ Know your *objective*
- ▶ Know your *target audience*
- ▶ Know the *product or service*

Your objective: What are you trying to accomplish? What response are you trying to obtain? Your objective might not be to make a sale, but rather to get your reader to send for free information or to get your reader to sign up for your mailing list. Or your objective might be to sell your product or service.

Your target audience: The more you know about your target audience, the easier it will be to convince them that they need your product or service. The more specific your knowledge of your target audience is, the better. Let's say you are selling a book on weight loss. Your target audience is overweight people, but you might fine-tune that to target overweight people whose jobs revolve around computer work and who have no time to work out, let alone go to the gym. This is the target audience of a website called WeightLossTricksThatWork.com. (See Figure 2.1.)

Your product or service: After identifying the audience to whom you are writing, it's essential to know the product or service about which you're writing. Immerse yourself in it. The five Ws of journalism are a handy tool to use for this: What? Why? Where? When? Who? and the bonus How? Before you begin writing, ask yourself:

What is the product or service? What is it made of?

Why was it invented or developed?

Where did it originate?

When was it discovered?

Who invented or discovered it?

How is it made?

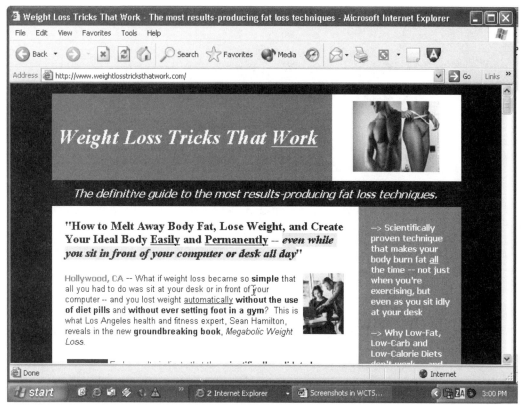

Figure 2.1 This targeted headline calls out to a specific audience.

Learn everything you can about your product or service. Uncover the *benefits* of owning your product or using your service. Only after you identify your objective, familiarize yourself with your target audience, and know your product or service thoroughly is it time to start writing.

CREATING THE BLUEPRINT: FIVE SIMPLE QUESTIONS YOU MUST ASK

▼

I've distilled the entire web copywriting process into five easy steps that make the task of writing web copy as easy as pie—and as enjoyable. Each step in the blueprint takes the form of a question. Once you answer each of the five questions about any product or service, you'll have the blueprint, a miniversion of your web copy. Note: As you are answering these five questions, *don't get creative*. Just answer factually. We'll get creative later.

Question 1. What Is the Problem?

Most sales, both online and offline, are based primarily on solving a problem. Having identified your target audience, your job now is to identify the problem that your target audience has that can be solved by your product or service. In copywriting terms these are known as the "three Ps"—pain, problem, or predicament.

This is where you play doctor. You diagnose the problem. The people in your target audience may not even know they have a problem, so it is your job to make them recognize it. Many web copywriters and marketers shove the solution down their viewers' throats before their readers recognize that there is a problem. That's like a doctor prescribing medicine *before* you feel sick or understand that the shot will prevent the flu.

There's another aspect to it as well. Once your audience understands they have a problem, you have to let them know that *you* understand their problem. There's an old saying that goes something like this: "People don't care how much you know until they know how much you care."

Step 1. *Write down your target audience's problem.* A few sentences will do. Your reader must be able to say, "Hey, she really understands my problem," or "He reads me like a book," or "She knows me so well it's as though she's been eavesdropping on my conversations or reading my mail." That's why I keep emphasizing that before you write a word of copy, you have to know your audience.

Question 2. Why Hasn't the Problem Been Solved?

Extending the doctor metaphor, this is where you further identify the history of the problem, predicament, or pain and look into the previous remedies or solutions that have been attempted but failed. As you progress through all five steps of this blueprint, you'll begin to see how the answer(s) to this question serves to build your audience's anticipation about a new solution you're about to reveal.

Step 2. *Write down the reason(s) why the problem continues, persists or lingers.* How is it that they haven't solved their problem, and why are they still stuck in the rut? Again, a few factual sentences will do.

Question 3. What Is Possible?

In coaching parlance, this is called *possibility thinking*. This is where you set the stage for what life could be like—what could happen—when your audience's problem, pain, or predicament is eliminated. You must go beyond stating the obvious. "The pain in your lower back will disappear," is not enough. You must draw a picture of what is possible now that the pain is gone. "You will be able to engage in activities [specify activities] you were unable to engage in because of your back pain," or "You can accomplish all your goals and dreams because the pain is no longer there to stop you." This is the dramatic promise.

Step 3. *Write down what's possible.* Paint a picture of the way things will be when your prospect's problems are solved. Again, a few sentences will do.

Question 4. What Is Different Now?

How will things change for your prospects? This is where you explain *who* you are and *how* your product or service can help them, as well as *what's* different about your product or service that will eliminate their problem. This is where your *unique selling proposition* (USP) comes in. A USP is something that sets you, your product or service, or your business apart from every other competitor in a *favorable* way. It's the *competitive advantage* that you proclaim to your prospects, customers, or clients.

Step 4. *Write a few sentences about what differentiates your product/service.* Present just the substance—not the details.

Question 5. What Should You Do Now?

If you answered the first four questions, and established your objective, you know what the answer to this question is. You simply tell your viewers to do what you started out wanting them to do—that is, to sign up, pick up the phone, register, opt-in, or buy the product or service you're selling.

Step 5. *State clearly what you want your prospect to do.* This is the call to action.

There you have it. Once you have answered the five questions, you have the blueprint for building your web copy. You now have the structure; all you have to do is decorate it. The fact is, with this blueprint alone, you can make some sales.

The Anatomy of the Blueprint

Recently, I had the opportunity to observe a business acquaintance named Ralph, a personal development coach, generate leads for his services during a Chamber of Commerce networking event. I noticed how successfully he was able to interest several people in his coaching services in such a small amount of time, so I took a closer look at how he could accomplish this with just a few words to each prospect. It didn't take long to realize that his sales pitch was nothing more than skillfully weaving the five steps of the blueprint into casual conversation. His conversations went something like this:

PROSPECT: What kind of work do you do, Ralph?

RALPH: I'm a personal development coach.

PROSPECT: Hmmm . . . what exactly is that?

RALPH: Let me ask you a question: Are there three things you'd like to accomplish in your life right now that for some reason or other you haven't been able to accomplish yet?

PROSPECT: Sure. I think I can think of more than three things.

RALPH: Why do you think you haven't been able to accomplish them?

PROSPECT: [Answers vary from person to person. They range from "I haven't focused enough attention on accomplishing them" to "I have an unsupportive boss/spouse/family" to "I can't seem to find the time or energy to devote to them" to "I'm stuck in a rut and I'm still trying to figure my way out of it," and so on.]

RALPH: What if you were able to eliminate [here, Ralph reiterates the challenge the prospect mentioned for not accomplishing his or her goals], how would your life change?

PROSPECT: [Again, answers to this question vary from person to person. "Why, I'd be able to spend more time with my family, and that would make me happy," or "I'd be able to work less and earn more," or "I'd have the money to buy a house/send my kids to college/go on more vacations," etc.]

> RALPH: What if I told you I have a unique approach to
> help you take care of [again, Ralph names the
> prospect's problem], which will help get you from
> where you are now to where you want to be—not in a
> few years, but within the next 60 to 90 days? Would
> you be interested in a 15-minute free consultation to
> find out how I can do that for you?
>
> PROSPECT: Sure, why not?

At this point, Ralph takes his business card out of his pocket
and asks what day and time would suit the prospect for the free
consultation. When the prospect answers, Ralph writes the
appointment on the card and hands the card to the prospect,
telling the prospect to call him at the appointed date and time.
He then turns the card over and points to a diagram on the
back.

> RALPH: Right before you call me, I'd like you to do some-
> thing fun. I'd like you to do this quick exercise here,
> tell me what your answer is when you call me, and I'll
> explain what your answer means.
>
> PROSPECT [LOOKING AT THE CARD]: Okay, you got it. I'll
> call you then.

Do you see what Ralph did? He managed to get a prospect
interested in his services in a matter of one or two minutes, and
he generated a lead that might eventually turn into a client,
which, of course, was his objective.

Let's examine the conversation more closely to see how it
relates to our blueprint. When prospects ask Ralph about his
work, Ralph uses it as an opportunity to identify their problems

(step 1). Instead of making an educated guess about what their problem(s) might be, he makes the prospects identify their problems by asking them to think of the top three things they have yet to accomplish. Then he asks why they haven't been able to accomplish them (step 2), and the prospects give specific reasons. Ralph next asks the what-if question; that is, he makes prospects imagine how life would be different if the problem(s) were eliminated (step 3). After his prospects answer the question, Ralph mentions his unique approach to helping them take care of the problem(s) so they can get from where they are in life to where they want to be in the next 60 to 90 days (step 4). This is followed up with an offer of a free 15-minute phone consultation at an appointed date and time (step 5). The fun exercise on the back of the card is a device Ralph employs to make sure prospects call him and to minimize no-shows.

Ralph's networking sales pitch is one small example of just how powerful the blueprint is. When you are able to successfully identify your prospect's problem and explain why the problem hasn't been solved, what's possible, what's different now, and what the prospect should do now, you have the basis of a direct response sales pitch in a nutshell. Although the blueprint works exceedingly well on the Internet, where web buyers' attention is difficult to capture, it can be applied to almost any situation that requires a direct response, both online or offline—from an "elevator speech" to a full-scale sales presentation.

Are you beginning to see how powerful the blueprint is? Do you think you can answer these five questions for any product or service you want to sell? If you answered yes, you're already a web copywriter.

Outstanding web copy starts with the five-step blueprint. Now let's examine how a website started out as a blueprint, was fleshed out into six pages of web copy that sold several hundred thousand dollars' worth of a product in a few months, and continues to sell to this day. The product is a $27 e-book that shows Internet entrepreneurs how to get free money from the government to start, grow, or expand their Internet businesses. The author is Matthew Lesko, who has written more than 70 books (including two *New York Times* bestsellers) showing everyday people how to get grants and free money from U.S. government sources. Before we look at the web copy, we'll take a look at the five-step blueprint upon which the copy was built:

Step 1. *What's the problem?* Internet entrepreneurs like you need money to start, grow, or expand your business.

Step 2. *Why hasn't the problem been solved?* Loans and financing for Internet businesses are hard to come by or qualify for. Free money programs, such as government grants, are neither advertised nor generally publicized—therefore, very few people know about them. The few who are aware of them lack the specialized knowledge of how to successfully obtain the free money.

Step 3. *What's possible?* Now you can get as much money as you need for your Internet business—and you don't have to pay it back.

Step 4. *What's different now?* The real trick is in knowing how to ask for the money. Matthew Lesko has developed a completely legal and ingenious secret formula that works every time. He discovered the secret formula because for the past 25 years, he has specialized in uncovering obscure government programs that most ordinary citizens know nothing about.

Step 5. *What should you do now?* Get the e-book that shows you step-by-step how to get your free money to which you're entitled.

That's it! End of blueprint.

Now take a look at the website at www.FreeStuffForEntrepreneursOnTheInternet.com, shown in Figure 2.2.

Every piece of web copy that I've written follows the same sequence and development set forth in the blueprint. Years of copywriting have made me instinctively structure my sales copy in that logical sequence. It wasn't always that way. When I first started writing copy, I would force-feed my brain with all manner of clever, innovative ways to craft my sales proposition—and usually ended up with volumes of words, research, and web copy that I later had to spend hours (sometimes days) chiseling down to a lean, mean selling machine. In other words, I was doing everything backward.

Then I devised this blueprint that made web copywriting a breeze. It is a loose adaptation of an executive summary template developed by my colleague and friend, Alex Mandossian, a web traffic conversion specialist, marketing consultant, and copywriter. I realized that if I started with this blueprint, which is the framework, and fleshed it out only as necessary, I came up with the same quality web copy that I'd been producing for years, but, using the blueprint, I slashed as much as 80 percent off the time it took to write copy.

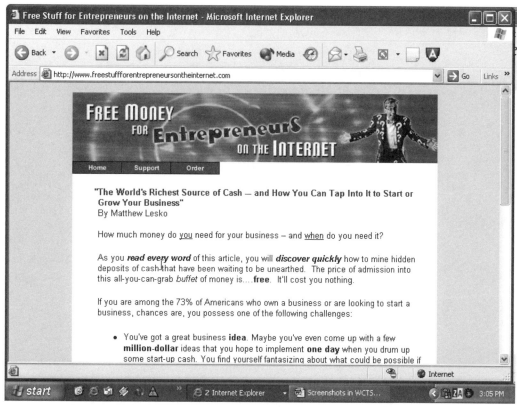

Figure 2.2 A fleshed-out version of the blueprint.

When you model success, you need to model the strategy, not the result (meaning you don't mimic someone else's writing style, you simply use the technique). The blueprint is one of the most important strategies that I can teach you. In my opinion, if you follow it, it's almost impossible to experience writer's block; and you won't have to put on the "writer's hat," so to speak. You won't struggle to be creative or clever or amusing or profound. You just write down the facts. Later, during the fleshing-out phase, you make those facts come alive.

PUTTING THE BLUEPRINT TO WORK:
FIVE EASY STEPS TO MAKING
YOUR WEB COPY SELL
▼

Let's suppose you've written down the five steps of the blueprint: You've identified the problem; you've described what's possible; you've established why the problem hasn't been solved; you've established what's changed; and you've suggested what action should be taken. What have you got? Is this your web copy? Obviously not, but it is the heart and soul—the framework—for writing web copy.

Some people will buy simply based on your answers to those five questions, but to get most people to buy, you must flesh out the blueprint until it becomes a virtual salesperson who sells for you day and night, 24/7, weekends and holidays, 365 days a year, without a vacation or sick leave.

You have created your blueprint. How do you build your house? As with the blueprint, there are five steps you need to take to flesh it out and make readers respond.

Step 1. Inject Emotion

I don't care how wonderful your vocabulary or how excellent your grammar is, if your words lack emotion, you won't sell a thing unless you can appeal to an emotion. Remember, *people buy on emotion and justify with logic.*

Injecting Emotion into the Problem. There are many ways to inject emotion. Here are a few examples:

- ▶ Does it frustrate you that your business is making only a small fraction of its profit potential?

- ▶ Doesn't it make you furious that you could actually be making five times as much (or more) from your existing business—if only you knew how?

- ▶ Don't you just get hopping mad every time you give a kick-ass sales presentation and your prospect *still* won't buy a thing from you?

- ▶ Do you feel paralyzed by the fear of rejection every time you have to ask that "cruel" prospect for the sale?

- ▶ Does your ego get clobbered whenever your prospect says no?

Injecting Emotion into What's Possible

- ▶ Imagine what your life would be like if all your debts were paid and you had triple-A credit?

- ▶ How would you like it if your business earned a five-figure income every month—even while the economy is on a downswing?

- ▶ What would it mean if you were the featured guest of popular radio and TV shows? Imagine thousands—potentially millions—of people hearing your story.

It's seven o'clock Monday morning. You're not really looking forward to another **grueling** week of selling, so you turn
on your computer. While you **sip your morning coffee,** you
watch Brian Tracy on RealVideo giving you 24 Techniques
for Closing the Sale in 63 minutes flat.

It's now 8:03 A.M., and you're feeling **unstoppable** and positively **empowered** because Brian Tracy has just given you a
personal coaching session that got you **charged up** with
everything you need **to get those sales.**

The next moment, you're out the door. You talk to your
first prospect, and moments later you make your first sale
with the **greatest of ease.** Feeling **high** on your victory, you
go on to your next prospect, and, again within moments,
you've got another sale in your pocket. No sweat! This goes
on all day long, and you **surprisingly** find yourself smiling
all the time. Gone are the stress and fear that you used to
have—and in their place is a deep-seated confidence that
you can **win over** any prospect you speak to. It's never been
this easy!

Then, toward the end of the day, you pick up the phone to
set up your future appointments. Every single prospect you
call says yes, they'd be happy to see you or talk to you this
week.

You think to yourself, "If only every day could be like
this . . . why, I might just earn a **six-figure income** this year."

Could this really happen to you? Don't be surprised if it
does.

Figure 2.3

Shown in Figure 2.3 is a device I call the *emotional scenario.* It paints a vivid picture of what it would be like for the reader to experience your product or service.

An emotional scenario such as this one accomplishes several things:

▶ It connects your reader to your product or service on an *emotional* level. Emotion sells.

▶ It assumes that the sale is already made.

▶ It allows the reader to take ownership of the product and have a *virtual experience* of it with excellent results.

Step 2. Add Bullet Points, Bonuses, Guarantee, and Close

The formula for writing bullets is first to state the benefit and then follow up by painting a picture of how your viewer's life will change when he or she gets that benefit or by elevating the desirability of that benefit by injecting emotion, drama, or intrigue. Bullets need to be powerful and tight.

Mouthwatering Bullets. Here are examples of great bullets (the first is an example of injecting emotion, drama, or intrigue; the second paints a picture):

▶ How to craft text links that are engaging—and highly clickable. Here, I reveal some of my jealously guarded devices, and I'm swearing you to secrecy on these.

▶ How a self-made millionaire invented this irresistible tactic. It virtually eliminates the need to close the sale because the sale will close itself for you—like a ripe apple dropping out of a tree into your hand.

I learned how to write bullets by studying and writing out by hand the bullets of great copywriters. You can do the same.

Bonuses. It is a widely accepted belief in direct marketing that significantly more sales are generated by an offer that includes a free bonus or gift. Although there aren't scientific studies that support this belief, it stands to reason that receiving attractive incentives creates a significantly greater desire to purchase the core product. It is not uncommon for people to buy a product primarily because of the freebies they get by buying the product. A "gifts with purchase" has become a staple in cosmetic counters everywhere because they significantly encourage impulse buying. Obviously, the bonus or gift must be desirable to the target audience and must relate in some way to the product or service being offered. If it has a dollar value worth noting, you should also mention that.

Free bonuses or gifts are particularly powerful when attached to a deadline for ordering, because the deadline injects urgency. You need to set a deadline to compel the reader to respond immediately instead of putting off the buying decision. That's where a dynamic date script is helpful. This is a small script that advances the deadline date displayed on your webpage every day. When people read your web copy, it looks something like this:

When you order the Memory Foam mattress pad by Sunday, April 11, 2004, you will also receive two (2) Memory Foam pillows absolutely free. These pillows are sold separately for $89.00 apiece, but they're yours *free* when you purchase a Memory Foam mattress.

The day and date advance by one day every day, automatically updating your deadline. Dynamic date scripts are widely available for free from various script sources on the web. You simply decide how many days into the future you'd like your prospect to act on your offer, and any web developer or programmer (or anyone who's familiar with html) can simply insert that into the script, and install the code into your webpage.

Guarantees.   Often, the sale is made with the promise of a money-back guarantee. This is where you eliminate the risk to the buyer and remove any remaining obstacles standing in the way of making a sale.

The Close.   Just because you have presented your offer doesn't mean your prospect will buy what you've offered. You have to close the sale. It's no different from visiting a store and looking at a product you are interested in buying; even after all your questions have been answered, until a salesperson closes the sale with a question like, "How would you like to pay for that?" the sale isn't made (unless you happen to be a highly motivated buyer, determined to buy that item then and there).

Before you ever ask for that order, it's essential that the prospect be primed for the close. The sequence of presenting copy elements (and hot buttons) is crucial. Unlike a store, where the price is out there for the buyer to see, in your web copy, you must wait until the end to reveal the price and ordering instructions. This puts your reader in the proper frame of mind to buy, because by the time you present the price, you would have laid out all the benefits and information your prospect needs. This is another way to keep the editorial feel of your web copy and not reveal your "hidden selling" too soon.

This is one of the reasons I do not put an order button on the left navigation bar of websites over which I have total control. If I've gone to a lot of trouble to make my web copy look like an editorial, I don't want to ruin that by putting an order button on the first screen, thereby removing all doubt that the editorial is actually an ad in disguise.

Another reason is that many web visitors click on the order button even before reading the web copy because they want to know what they are getting themselves into and whether or not they want what you're offering. If they click before they read, the order page then determines whether visitors read your web copy or not. It defeats the purpose of your copy, which is to use the power of your copy to get readers happily involved with your product or service.

In addition, an order button allows people to make a judgment about the price before knowing the details of your offer. If I had an order button on my Web Copywriting University website, for instance, and you clicked on it and found that my course costs $997, would you read my web copy? The bottom line is, few people are predisposed to spend that much money until they understand the value of what they are getting for that investment.

One of the major mistakes website owners make is that they fail to close the sale. They go to great lengths to get people to visit their websites, and they do everything possible to make a compelling selling argument about their product or service, but at the last moment, when the prospect is just about ready to buy, they drop the ball and fail to ask for the order. Unsuccessful marketers are reluctant to ask for the order. For any offer to be successful, you must be clear and explicit when you ask for the order. Include every detail, even those that seem obvious to you. Make it easy for the prospect to buy.

What Does It Take to Close a Sale?   Online or offline, simply asking for the order does *not* close the sale. "Click here to order" or similar phrases do *not* constitute a close. As a rule, web visitors click on the order button only after you have done the necessary steps to close the sale. If you haven't given enough information, you haven't closed the sale. Period.

Closing the sale starts on the home page—usually as early as the first or second screen. Those of you who have sold offline know that clinching the sale often takes several trial closes leading up to the final close. Just like a real-life salesperson, your cyberspace salesperson (i.e., your website) should contain trial closes. If you look at the website shown in Figure 2.4, you'll see that I used eight closes to sell the software program.

You must always remember that people's *buying decision times vary*. Some people are ready to buy after they have found a benefit or two, and some aren't ready to buy until they've read every word on the website. For this reason, you have to catch them at every point at which they're likely to buy.

---

8 Trial Closes (and 1 Final Close) Were Used to Sell *Sculptor 3*

Note: Underlined words are text links that lead to the order page.

1) I've shown you how *Sculptor 3* uses computerization to literally immerse you in 7 of the top manifesting technologies simultaneously—and materialize your desires faster than you ever thought possible. Now, it's time for you to <u>act on this</u>.

2) Well, the good news is that you can own *Sculptor 3* for less than $100! Yes, that's right. Valuable as it is, *Sculptor 3* can be yours for a one-time investment of just $97 (USD). If you're in a hurry and can't wait to get started, click here to <u>experience *Sculptor 3* now</u>.

3) <u>Get started</u> creating your ideal life now.

4) So you have nothing to lose when you <u>give it a try</u> today. Within minutes, you will get download instructions, and you can start enjoying the benefits of *Sculptor 3* immediately.

5) To give you an even better value on your *Sculptor 3* investment, you'll also get 7 FREE gifts valued at $127 when you order <u>right now</u>.

6) Remember, I can't guarantee that you'll receive the 7 FREE gifts above unless you order *Sculptor 3* right now.

7) With *Sculptor 3*, you don't have to learn anything. Instead, it can do all the work for you—making it easy to apply manifesting principles to your life and helping you get what you want the easy and effective way. <u>Get started now</u>.

8) Imagine ... in as little as a few days or weeks, you could be manifesting the life you've always dreamed of. Imagine being totally debt-free, enjoying improved health ... happy and loving relationships ... your dream house ... all because you decided to say "YES" today.

9) Final Close:

Click to ORDER Via Our SECURE SERVER!

Figure 2.4 Several attempts to close the sale are necessary for successful web selling (www.affirmware.com.au).

Step 3. Add Credibility-Building Elements

If you've immersed yourself in your product or service, you have probably uncovered testimonials, interesting stories or case studies, significant facts, quotes or statistics related to your product or service. If for some reason you haven't, you can do speedy research on the web to fill in the gaps.

Again, for examples of these, all you have to do is take a look at my web copywriting samples—particularly the ones enclosed in boxes. See the stories that pull people in, the testimonials that support and strengthen the selling proposition, the interesting stories that both inform and whet my reader's appetite for what I have to offer, etc. For specific examples, go to www.PsychologicalTriggers.com, www.BreakthroughsJournal. com, www.FreeStuffForEntrepreneursOnTheInternet.com.

How to Use a Search Engine to Do Rapid Research. Advertising Age's website (www.adage.com) named David Ogilvy as one of the Top 100 players in advertising history, in part because of the way Ogilvy "created clean, powerful ads marked by graceful, sensible copy and a palpable respect for the consumer's intelligence." In his book, *Confessions of an Advertising Man*, Ogilvy wrote: "In my first Rolls-Royce advertisement I used 719 words—piling one fascinating fact on another." This technique is also perfect for the web. Long copy, particularly when used on a webpage, needs fascinating facts, figures, stories, or anecdotes that keep your visitors glued to your webpage until they read your offer and act on it.

Copernic Agent Basic is a free search engine tool that facilitates the task of finding information you need to flesh out your copy. Finding interesting anecdotes, stories, case studies, significant facts, quotes, and statistics is easy with this powerful search engine tool. Most of the fascinating facts I've included in web copy I've written over the years came from web searches done on Copernic Agent Basic. Particularly when the subject matter is bland or lifeless and needs an injection of excitement (to keep the readers reading), I turn to this tool for help.

When you type in the key words or key phrases of any topic you're looking for, Copernic generates the top ten results of the top ten search engines, and it even removes duplicate entries.

So your search results are a lot more relevant than if you had used only one search engine at a time.

There is so much on the web that you'll never run out of interesting angles or writing ideas, but do be careful; some information on the web is not reliable. Be sure you know your sources. Copernic is one of my writing secrets. You can download Copernic Agent Basic for free at Copernic.com.

Step 4. Add Psychological Devices

This is such an important and complex topic that I'll be devoting all of Chapter 3 to it. Among the topics we examine are the following:

- ▶ A persuasion device that gets people to commit to the sale

- ▶ Involvement devices to get readers to read every word of your copy

- ▶ Hypnotic commands and how to embed them into your copy

- ▶ Specific words you can plant in your web copy that make your readers believe what you say

- ▶ Commands that bypass your readers' conscious minds and overcome resistance

Step 5. Replace Rational Words with Emotional Words

You probably have heard the concept of right-brain and left-brain functions: The left hemisphere of the brain is the rational, logical, organized, analytic, linear, critical side; the right hemisphere is the creative, emotional, intuitive side, the realm of the imagination. Since people buy on emotion, the more you appeal to the right side of the brain, the more you'll sell. You do this by using emotional words, not intellectual, rational, bland, and boring words. Here are a few examples:

Use the words *speed up* instead of *accelerate*.

Instead of saying *accolade* use *applause*.

Use *rich* instead of *wealthy*.

Say *worried* instead of *concerned*.

Instead of saying *The following are . . .* , say *Here are . . .*

Try this: Take a look at the list of left-brain and right-brain words in Figure 2.5. Next, look at the web copy you've written, identify any left-brain (or rational) words, and replace those left-brain words with the right-brain (or emotional) words. How can I make it simpler than that?

Paul Galloway, an Internet programmer, created a neat little Common Gateway Interface (CGI) script to automatically replace all instances of left-brain (rational) words on any website with right-brain (emotional) words. A CGI script is a small program that takes data from a web server and does something with it; in this case, it replaces certain words from one database

Left-Brain (Rational) Words/Phrases	Right-Brain (Emotional) Words/Phrases	Left-Brain (Rational) Words/Phrases	Right-Brain (Emotional) Words/Phrases
accelerate	speed up	intelligent	bright
accolade	applause	I regret	I'm sorry
additionally	here's more/there's more	jesting	joking
aid	help	large	big
allow	let	learn	find out
anticipate	expect	manufacture	make
astute	smart	notion	idea
at an end	over	nude	naked
attractive	good looking	observed	seen
avid	eager	obstinate	stubborn
beneficial	good for	omit	leave out
challenge	dare	perceive	see
circular	round	perhaps	maybe
combat	fight	peril	danger
completed	finished	perspiration	sweat
concerned	worried	pleased	happy
concerning	about	preserve	save
construct	build	prevent	stop
courageous	brave	purchase	buy
demise	death	propitious	favorable
difficult	tough/hard	receive	get
diminutive	small	requested	ask for
disclose	reveal/explain	reply	answer
donate	give	select	pick/choose
elderly	old	soiled	dirty
facilitate	ease	stomach	belly
famished	hungry	strike	hit
fatigued	tired	subsequent to	since
fearful	afraid	sufficient	enough
following is/are	here's/here are	superior	better
for	because	tardy	late
fortunate	lucky	terminate	end
futile	hopeless	tidings	news
gratification	enjoyment	utilize	use
hasten	hurry	wealthy	rich
huge	giant	youthful	young
humorous	funny		
ill	sick		
immediately	right now		
inform	tell		

Figure 2.5 Left-brain versus right-brain expressions.

acclaimed, amazingly simple, announcing, appetizing, astonishing,
   automatically
booming, breakthrough
cash in, critical
discover, does the trick
easy-to-follow, enhanced, electrifying, exciting, exclusive, exponential
fantastic, fascinating, first, free
generous, good-as-gold, guaranteed
how-to
improved, incredible, initial, introducing
limited offer, love
handy, high-voltage, honest-to-goodness
immaculate, in-depth, ingenious, innovative, instantly, intensity, invaluable,
   irresistible
legendary
megawatt, mouthwatering
never been easier, new, no-holds-barred
one-stop shopping, outstanding, overwhelming
phenomenal, pioneer, powerful, proven techniques
rack up profits, rejuvenating, renewed, renowned, reproducible, revealed,
   revolutionary
satisfying, secrets, serene, shocking, skilled, special, spectacular, startling,
   step-by-step, successful, super
tactic, tempting, time-sensitive, trailblazing, trick
ultimate, unbeatable, unforgettable, uninhibited, unique, unlimited, urgent
within minutes, wonderful
you

Figure 2.6 Web words and phrases that sell.

(rational words) with corresponding words from another database (emotional words).

   If you go to www.paulgalloway.com/cgi-bin/emotional_
words.cgi and type in the URL of your website, it will show

your website with all the rational words displayed in red, followed by the suggested emotional word you might want to replace them with.

Take a look, too, at the list of web words and phrases that sell in Figure 2.6.

Tip: Replace the word *if* with *when* whenever you are describing what people will get from you. This is part of *assuming that the sale is made.*

REINFORCING THE FRAMEWORK: A SUMMARY
▼

First, *identify* your objective and your target audience; then get to know your product or service thoroughly.

Second, *create* your blueprint by answering the following five questions:

1. What's the problem?

2. Why hasn't the problem been solved?

3. What's possible?—(the promise)

4. What's different now?

5. What should you do now?

Third, *flesh out* your web copy by taking the blueprint and

1. Injecting emotion into it

2. Adding bullet points, bonuses, the guarantee, and the close

3. Adding credibility-building elements such as testimonials, interesting stories or case studies, significant facts,
   quotes, or statistics

4. Adding psychological devices (more about these in the
   next chapter)

5. Replacing all rational words with emotional words

3

From Prospects to Purchasers:
The Psychological Motivators

Since 95 percent of people are imitators and only 5 percent initiators, people are persuaded more by the actions of others than by any proof we can offer.
—Cavett Roberts

Step 4 of our blueprint called for adding the psychological devices that transform readers into *buyers*. These are tactics that fly beneath the radar of your readers' perception, producing an almost *hypnotic effect* that actually makes them want to buy what you are selling— often without knowing why. These devices are extremely powerful, and if used inappropriately, can be dangerous. I urge you to use them discreetely, responsibly, and ethically.

Using psychology to sell is *not* about conning people into giving you their hard-earned money. It's *not* about manipulating people to do something against their will. It *is* about using your understanding of human nature to make your readers voluntarily and willingly become happily involved in a buying decision that you have made painless, even enjoyable. The fact is that all the psychological devices and triggers in the world won't amount to anything if you fail to speak to the needs of your target audience—and your target audience's *frame of mind*.

THE "REASON WHY" DEVICE

In his book, *Influence: The Psychology of Persuasion*, Robert Cialdini, Ph.D., discussed an experiment conducted by Harvard social psychologist Ellen Langer in which she demonstrated that people like to have a *reason* for doing something. Her experiment was simple. People were waiting in line to use a copy machine at a library. Langer's colleague asked those waiting if she could go ahead of them, saying, "Excuse me, I have five pages. May I use the Xerox machine because I'm in a rush?" Interestingly, 94 percent of those asked, complied. Note the word *because* that introduced a reason for the request.

The experiment was repeated with a new group. This time Langer's colleague said, "Excuse me, I have five pages. May I use the Xerox machine?" Only 60 percent agreed, a significant decrease. When the requester did not offer a reason, significantly fewer people complied.

They repeated the experiment a third time, saying, "Excuse me, I have five pages. May I use the Xerox machine, because I have to make some copies?" Although the reason was not a convincing one (*everyone* in line had to make copies), 93 percent of those asked said yes. Just the semblance of a reason introduced by the word *because* was enough to persuade people to comply.

In selling a product or service, always tell your readers why they need to do what you're asking them to do. Something as simple as "You must act now because this offer expires on December 31, after which we can no longer accept orders" is sufficient.

THE ZEIGARNIK EFFECT ▼

There is a phenomenon called the *Zeigarnik effect* named after the Gestalt theorist. It represents that state of mental tension and unbalance caused by uncompleted tasks.

When applied to writing web copy, it means that you shouldn't litter your website with a slew of subjects and topics that will distract your reader. It means that you must stick to a single message so that you can lead readers down your intended sales path. This is the "linear path" method of writing web copy.

To understand this better, think of the psychology of a website visitor: When web visitors arrive at your site, they scan through the entire site looking for things that interest them. If several buttons and links grab their attention, they make a mental note of them and start reading the one that interests them most. Now, here's the interesting thing: While they are reading that page, the Zeigarnik effect takes over, creating that mental tension that comes from uncompleted tasks, which, in the case of your visitor, is the urge to click on those other buttons or links.

Since the brain is unable to pay full attention to the topic at hand until those other tasks are completed, this can create a problem, especially if you happen to be in the middle of making a selling proposition when the effect takes over. Not only will you lose your readers' attention, it is unlikely they will go down your intended sales path or take action of any kind, because their brain is compelling them to do the other tasks. That's why it's advisable to minimize the number of unnecessary links and buttons on your website in order to keep your reader on the linear path.

Likewise, mental tension may appear when, in the course of reading your copy, your reader comes across unfamiliar concepts or terms. To combat this, I employ small pop-up windows to explain concepts that might create mental tension. That way, readers can click on the link, quickly relieve the tension by reading the brief explanation in the pop-up window, and continue reading what I want them to read. The other way, they might be tempted to click away, never to return.

The linear path concept and the Zeigarnik effect are both very powerful concepts that many web copywriters and website owners fail to understand. If you're ever tempted to include advertising banners on your website, or reciprocal links with other websites, or links to other unrelated pages in your website that don't contribute to the sales process, remember that you are violating the linear path concept and allowing the Zeigarnik effect to kick in.

THE CLIFFHANGER PRINCIPLE ▼

The Cliffhanger principle is one of my favorite devices. If you've ever watched the season finale of a TV series, or heard teasers for TV news or newsmagazines that say things like, "Is green tea the new miracle cure for cancer? Film at eleven," you already understand the concept.

This is a variation of the Zeigarnik effect. The uncompleted thought demands our attention. As a result, we eagerly sit in front of our TV sets to see the season premiere of our favorite shows just to find out what happens next, or listen to an entire news broadcast just to hear that 30-second snippet that answers the question that's been bugging our brain.

You can imagine the impact this principle has on web copy. Whenever I break my copy into multiple webpages and it's essential that readers click through to the next page, I use a cliffhanger to get them to click. For example, here is the copy I wrote as the last paragraph of a webpage. "The secret ingredient of branding that can single-handedly turn a small business enterprise into a mega-success is hidden in Tommy Hilfiger's story. Did you catch it? Here it is . . ." (followed by a button marked "Next Page").

NEUROLINGUISTIC PROGRAMMING (NLP) ▼

Neurolinguistic programming is the science of how the brain codes learning and experience. This coding affects all communication and behavior. NLP involves the use of proper syntax (or language). Using it properly can make all your written communications more persuasive. There are several NLP devices that I often use in writing web copy. Among them are embedded commands, presuppositions, linguistic binds, and reframing.

Embedded Commands

Web copywriting is direct-response writing, which means that its objective is to generate a response of some kind, such as getting your readers to pick up the phone and call your business, subscribe to your newsletter, sign up for your mailing list, or buy your product or service. Using embedded commands entails crafting the action you want your reader to take and wrapping it in the cushion of a casual, innocent-looking sentence.

Consider the following sentence:

I wonder how quickly *you are going to buy this product?*

It seems harmless enough. Your reader might consciously take it as a hypothetical comment. But notice the embedded command, which is quite hypnotic in effect:

. . . you are going to buy this product.

Using embedded commands in speaking calls for altering your tone of voice. You would lower your voice and speak the command part of the sentence more slowly for emphasis and to produce a hypnotic effect.

In writing, however, you use the boldface type (or quotation marks, or italics, or a different color) to set off or delineate your command. When you write, "I wonder how quickly you are going to buy this product," use boldface type for the command, "**you are going to buy this product.**" The bold type plays a role in how effectively the command is communicated. A person will respond to that part of the sentence as a command, and will follow the command without consciously realizing it.

In this way, you *gain compliance effortlessly.* Your readers don't even perceive that they've been given a command. Typically, they will obey your command as though they had received it directly, without any resistance whatsoever. Clearly, this is a very powerful tool. Because embedded commands evade the scrutiny of the left brain (the critical, logical side of the brain), the readers are not aware of what is causing their desire.

Embedded commands motivate people to take action and compel readers to come to a quick decision. Advertisers have known this for years, and that is why they write slogans like, "Aren't you glad you use Dial? Don't you wish everybody did?" The embedded command, of course, is "use Dial." The same is true of, "Wouldn't you really rather have a Buick?" Of course, the embedded command used in the sentence is "have a Buick."

How to Write an Embedded Command. Start by constructing your command. This is usually three to seven words articulated in the *imperative voice;* that is, you begin with an action verb that presupposes the subject "you."

Examples of commands

Get your hands on this [name product].

Act on my advice.

Say yes to this offer.

Learn this secret.

Pick up the phone.

Next, simply embed the command in a sentence and set it off in bold type. For example, if the action you want your readers to take is to "read every word of this article," your sentence could read, "*As you read every word of this article,* you will discover advanced psychological tactics that will boggle your mind."

Presuppositions

Powerful as the brain is, it usually can focus on only one major thing at a time. Therefore, when bombarded by multiple thoughts, it is forced to presuppose (assume) and accept suggestions as facts. This is why using presuppositions in your web copy is such a powerful technique.

The question, "What will you do with the extra $2,500 you'll earn next month?" is an example of a presupposition. Your brain is asked the question, "What will you do . . . ?" By its very nature, the human brain is compelled to answer it. It's an involuntary, spontaneous reaction. When your brain is asked a question, it instantly goes to work in search of an answer. If you've ever had the experience of waking up in the middle of the night with the answer to a question you were thinking about earlier in the day, then you've experienced the profound effect questions have on the brain. The brain will keep working on the question subconsciously until it comes up with an answer (if not verbally, then mentally). The answer may not always be correct, but the brain will be satisfied only when it has produced an answer that it considers valid.

The question, "What will you do with the extra $2,500 you'll earn next month?" assumes that you will earn $2,500 next month simply by asking what you're going to do with it. This is called an *adjacency pair* in NLP parlance, and the reader's/listener's brain pays attention only to the first part ("What will you do . . .") of the pair. A significant percentage of language processing takes place subconsciously. To understand a question or sentence, we must *subconsciously* make assumptions in order to make sense of what is being asked or said. Therefore, in order to answer the question, your brain has to assume that the second part of the question "the extra $2,500 you'll earn next month" is an established fact. Do you see how smoothly that just slides into your consciousness?

Presuppositions are often seen in the leading questions so prevalent in courtroom dramas. These leading questions imply the existence of something when, in fact, its existence has not been established. Consider the following question:

"Why did you steal the money?"

The question assumes the existence of a sum of money. It further assumes that the money has been stolen, that "you" have stolen it, and that you have a reason for having stolen it ("Why"?). When questions such as these are delivered by a lawyer skilled in the syntax of presuppositions—especially when fired in rapid succession (*stacked presuppositions*), the listener is often forced to tacitly accept the *implied* meaning of the questions, even when the adversarial questioning was designed to introduce damaging arguments.

Here's another example of a presupposition: What will you do when the government imposes a five-cent surcharge on every e-mail that you send out? The brain focuses on the first part of the adjacency pair ("What will you do . . ."), which means it has to presuppose that the latter part of the sentence (about the government imposing a five-cent surcharge on every e-mail that you send out) is an established fact, when it actually is nothing but a rumor.

Here's another example: "Are you one of the 295 million people in America who's tired of the nine to five corporate grind, who wants to start her own business?" The question presupposes that there are 295 million people who want to start their own business in America, when that fact hasn't been established. Heck, that figure even exceeds the total population of the United States!

Not all presuppositions come in the form of questions. You can use presuppositional phrases like "As you know," "I'm sure you know," "Everybody knows . . ." and presuppositional words like "clearly," "obviously," "evidently," "undoubtedly," "easily," "readily," "automatically," and "naturally." Any statement you put after any of these words is more likely to be received or accepted by your reader without resistance. For example, "Obviously, these triggers usher in a revolutionary—and immensely more effective—era of selling that you simply can't miss out on," or "Clearly, investing in Adam Ginsberg's program, *Creating a Successful eBay Business,* is the fastest way to start earning eBay profits in as little as one day.

"Clearly" and all the other presuppositional words and phrases impart a halo of credibility around what you are saying and lead the reader to assume that the ensuing statement is true. It makes the statement take on the *appearance* of fact and therefore makes your sales argument go down smoothly.

I am not suggesting that you use this device to tell lies, use weasel words, or slip your readers a Mickey. I believe in telling the truth in advertising. As with any powerful psychological device, you have to use presuppositions ethically and judiciously.

Linguistic Binds

A linguistic bind is a form of syntax that makes your reader say, "Why, of course, what you're saying is true!" and is another powerful tool in the art of persuasion. Let's analyze this linguistic bind: "While you're sitting there reading this letter, you begin to understand why you can't afford to waste any more time getting less than everything that life has to offer."

It consists of two parts. Part 1 states something obvious ("you're sitting there reading this letter"), and part 2 states what you want your reader to think, say, or do. It is the command. Curiously, this pattern makes your reader believe that what you are saying is logical, when in fact, parts 1 and 2 of your sentence are not linked by logic at all. Nevertheless, this device can make people agree with practically anything you say.

Here are some more examples of linguistic binds:

"Now that you've read this special report, I'm sure you realize that you need to beat your competitors to the punch by attending this seminar now."

"As you sit there reading this, I know that you're thinking about all the ways you can turn your book into a bestseller as a result of attending Mark Victor Hansen's Book Marketing University."

"As you think about what you really need in your business, you begin to realize that you have only one choice to make, and that is to invest in this [product or service]."

There are other variations of linguistic binds. One is *"The more you A, the more you B" syntax*. For example:

"The more you understand the power of this one psychological trigger, the more you'll realize that you need to get all 30 of Joe Sugarman's Psychological Triggers."

"The more you read, the more you won't want to be without this incredible product."

Another is the *cause-and-effect syntax:* "Taking advantage of this free trial of our water purifier in the comfort of your own home will cause you to fully understand why buying bottled water is simply not the way to go."

Again, I caution you to use this powerful device judiciously and ethically.

Reframing

Reframing is the process of altering one's perception of a person, place, or thing by changing the context in which it is viewed. Consider *reframing* in its literal sense. Imagine a piece of canvas on which paint has been splattered, dripped, dabbed, and flicked in a chaotic manner, and then imagine hanging that canvas on a wall in a plain metal frame. You would most likely view it as just one big mess. Now imagine that same piece of canvas reframed in an ornate museum-quality, solid-hardwood frame with custom moldings. Suddenly, you perceive it as a work of art.

Our perception of a person, place or thing is altered simply by changing the context—the frame—in which it is viewed. In verbal or written communication, perception can be altered by using a technique known as *reframing*.

Reframing in the context of copywriting is a technique for communicating a flaw, a shortcoming, an imperfection, or a disadvantage in a way that transforms its meaning to one that is pleasant, desirable, or advantageous. Advertisers often abuse this concept by saying misleading things like, "When you purchase this camera, you will also get as a free gift this genuine, handsome, imitation-leather carrying case." There is nothing genuine about imitation leather. *Don't* reframe in this way because it will insult the intelligence of your audience.

The key to successful reframing is to shift the reader's focus to a desirable, sometimes hidden, aspect of a disadvantage and turn it into a plus. You may be surprised to discover how just about anything can be reframed into something desirable when you look at it in a different light or, more accurately, with a fresh set of eyes.

Reframing is an excellent tool to use to justify the price of what you're selling. In the following example, reframing was used to justify the $1,595 price tag for a one-day speakers' workshop:

What price can you put on learning how to get as many speaking engagements as you can handle? $25,000? $15,000? $10,000? (Believe it or not, that's how much other speaker trainers charge!)

If you paid me my standard consulting fee of $625/hour for the 7½ hours I'm giving you at the Speakers' Workshop on October 18, it would cost you $4,687.50.

Would you believe it if I told you the workshop won't even cost you $4,000? No, not even $3,000. Your investment in your speaking career—*and* your life—is only . . .

$1,595.

You'll most likely earn at least **twice** that much on **your very first speaking engagement.**

Here, the price of the workshop ($1,595) is compared to: (1) how much other speaker trainers charge ($25,000, $15,000, or $10,000); (2) the cost in consulting fees to receive an equivalent 7½ hours of training ($4,687.50); and (3) how much the buyer would earn on his or her first speaking engagement (twice as much as the price of tuition to attend the speakers' workshop). When reframed in this context, what could appear to be a prohibitive amount of money to spend on a one-day workshop suddenly seems reasonable—even inexpensive.

THE COMMITMENT/CONSISTENCY ELEMENT OF INFLUENCE

▼

One extremely powerful and seductive device I use frequently is the commitment/consistency element of influence that I learned from Robert Cialdini. Human beings have a nearly obsessive desire to be—or to appear—consistent to others and to ourselves. Once we've subscribed to something, voted for something, bought something, or taken a stand on something, we are under tremendous pressure to behave consistently with that commitment in order to justify our earlier decision.

I use this "element of influence" technique in writing web copy by first helping my reader express a firm stand or opinion about something, then presenting my product in a way that it plays to the stand my reader has taken. I first construct a question to which the reader could not possibly answer no, such as, "If I could show you a way to double or triple your sales closing rate—and teach you how to sell 50 to 100 percent of all prospects you come in contact with—are you willing to spend an entertaining 63 minutes to learn it?"

By asking this question, I have, in effect, extracted an unspoken commitment from the readers, even if I receive no audible reply. Next, I tell them to read the rest of the article, where I give the details of my offer. After I've given the sales pitch, I say something like,

> Earlier on, I asked you the question: "If I could show you a way to double or triple your sales closing rate—and

teach you how to sell 50 to 100 percent of all prospects you come in contact with—are you prepared to spend 63 minutes to learn it?"

Since you're still reading this, I'm going to assume you answered, "Yes." Well, now that I've shown you unequivocally how Brian Tracy's 24 Techniques for Closing the Sale can deliver on that promise—and have also shown you Brian's first-rate credentials and the rave reviews he's received—it's time for you to act on this."

As you can see, I remind readers that they need to behave consistently with the commitment they've made. This is one of the most powerful weapons of influence.

COGNITIVE DISSONANCE ▼

The best way to explain the concept of cognitive dissonance is to tell you a story—actually, a fable. You probably remember this Aesop's fable. There once was a fox who tried in vain to reach a cluster of grapes dangling from a vine above his head. Although the fox leaped high to grasp the grapes, the delicious-looking fruit remained just beyond his reach. After several attempts, the fox gave up and said to himself, "These grapes are sour, and if I had some, I would not eat them."

This fable illustrates what former Stanford University social psychologist Leon Festinger called *cognitive dissonance*. Cognitive dissonance is the distressing mental state in which people "find themselves doing things that don't fit with what they know, or having opinions that conflict with other opinions they hold."

The fox's withdrawal from the pursuit of the grapes clashed with his thinking that the grapes were tasty. By changing his attitude toward the grapes, however, he was able to maintain an acceptable explanation for his behavior.

You can put this to effective use in your web copy by giving your readers a compelling reason to buy early in the sales process. This, in turn, will make them more likely to buy when confronted with the actual buying decision. Your readers have to be able to take ownership of that promise and cling to it so tenaciously that no other thought can pry it away from them. Any doubts or obstacles that may occur to them during the sales process will be overcome by the original belief, paving the way to a home-run sale.

Cialdini wrote about a presentation he attended where two presenters tried to recruit new members into the Transcendental Meditation program. The presentation began with a compelling selling argument. However, when it came to the question-and-answer portion, an attendee demolished the presenters' arguments, and the presentation collapsed. The rest of the audience, however, instead of being turned off, rushed in record numbers to plunk down their $75 deposit to attend the TM program.

Cialdini thought that the other attendees hadn't quite understood the arguments or the logic of the dissenting attendee, but after interviewing those who signed up, he learned that they had had good reasons for considering signing up for the TM program *before* attending the presentation. Apparently, the dissenter's remarks, instead of dissuading them, compelled them to sign up; otherwise, they might go home, think about the dissenter's arguments, and never sign up, which would have contradicted their original commitment to TM.

Driven by their needs, they were desperately searching for a way to solve their problems, and they very much wanted to believe that TM was their answer. Rather than face the tedious task of finding another solution to their problems, they opted for the comfort of staying with their original belief despite evidence to the contrary.

How can you use cognitive dissonance in your web copy? In the beginning of your web copy, you have to get your reader to say, "Yes, that's exactly what I need!" You can do this by crafting a *well-articulated promise* and inserting it very early in the body copy. Next, get readers to take ownership of that promise and cling to it so tenaciously that no one can pry it away from them. That way, any doubts or obstacles that may arise during the sales process will be squashed by the original belief, thus paving the way to clinching the sale. Here are examples of well-articulated promises:

By the time you finish reading this article, you will know how to *consistently pick the hottest stocks* that are on the *upswing* right now—so you can make a killing on the stock market every time.

What if I told you I could show you how to *increase your ability to ethically influence others,* naturally, *without sounding like you're making a sales pitch.* How much more money and success could you create with that skill?

INVOLVEMENT DEVICES THAT
MULTIPLY SALES
▼

Involvement devices are devices that get people involved with your copy. They move people to read every word of your copy. Getting your website visitors to read your copy is job number one if your objective is to sell them something. When you use involvement devices, you effectively own your audience; that is, you hold your audience captive.

I tested an involvement device on the website of a client who sells affirmation software. This client's web copy had a decent conversion rate, so I rewrote his copy and added the involvement device shown in Figure 3.1. I installed this involvement device in the first screen of my client's website, and his sales tripled the next day. During subsequent weeks, he maintained sales that were 200 to 300 percent more than the previous daily sales (he even had days when he sold six times as much product as he had previously).

The original headline, "Learn how to be prosperous, successful and happy in just 10 minutes a day," was an attempt to get at what he thought were the hot buttons of his target audience, but, although reasonably successful, the headline sounded vague, and it definitely was *not* riveting. It didn't call out to the real desires of his target audience.

The involvement device asked readers to identify their wants, needs, and dreams. What could be more riveting to your target audience than their specific dreams, the dreams they might not dare tell another living soul? The involvement device

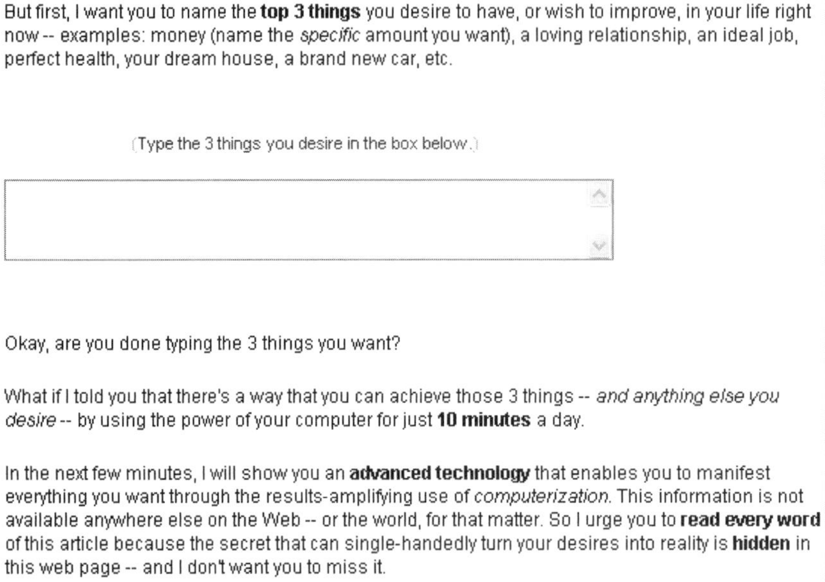

But first, I want you to name the **top 3 things** you desire to have, or wish to improve, in your life right now -- examples: money (name the *specific* amount you want), a loving relationship, an ideal job, perfect health, your dream house, a brand new car, etc.

(Type the 3 things you desire in the box below.)

Okay, are you done typing the 3 things you want?

What if I told you that there's a way that you can achieve those 3 things -- *and anything else you desire* -- by using the power of your computer for just **10 minutes** a day.

In the next few minutes, I will show you an **advanced technology** that enables you to manifest everything you want through the results-amplifying use of *computerization*. This information is not available anywhere else on the Web -- or the world, for that matter. So I urge you to **read every word** of this article because the secret that can single-handedly turn your desires into reality is **hidden** in this web page -- and I don't want you to miss it.

Figure 3.1 Example of an involvement device.

asked them to name their dreams, and it gave them a safe place to do it because they knew that no one would ever see their response. Bringing the readers' desires into focus allowed us to present the product (affirmation software) as the means of achieving those desires.

Do you see how powerful that is? Involvement devices break people's preoccupation with other things. At any given moment, a people's attention is occupied with dozens of things—everything from how they're going to pay for their children's college education to what they're going to have for dinner that night. Think of your prospect's mind as an antenna that receives signals from everywhere. Like a radio tuner, an involvement device gets people tuned in to only one signal, one station, or one channel—in this case, *your* sales message or your web copy. Getting someone's attention on the Internet is probably the biggest challenge you face, because attention is in short supply—with over 4 billion webpages clamoring for attention.

In an effort to capture attention in the overwhelming marketplace that is the Internet, an increasing number of websites in various industries have begun to employ involvement devices. For instance, I've seen a retailer of loudspeakers feature a Home Theater Wizard on its website. The Home Theater Wizard is simply an involvement device that asks a few simple questions of the web visitor, about budget, room characteristics, listening preferences, and equipment setup. The web visitor clicks on check boxes to answer the brief questionnaire, thereby becoming effectively involved. Based on the answers given, the Home Theater Wizard recommends one of the company's preconfigured home theater systems customized to the customer's wants and needs. Since there's no way the company could know what web visitors are looking for in a home theater system, and it offers more than 350 different combinations of speakers from which to choose, the involvement device gets visitors to participate in customizing a system for their needs. In the process, the device causes casual web visitors to stay in the website (instead of clicking away) and take a close look at the website's product offerings.

Amazon.com has a Jewelry & Watches division that employs a similar involvement device. Its website uses a wizard that enables visitors to create a diamond ring to their specifications by answering four questions (visitors click on radio buttons to select their preferred shape, number of carats, type of metal for the setting, and the setting style). When a web visitor answers all four questions, he or she can preview the ring, then select the diamond quality and ring size. The wizard recommends a ring from the jewelry inventory and gives the price of the ring and ordering instructions. This is a more effective approach to choosing a diamond ring than viewing hundreds or thousands that are available.

Figure 3.2 shows an example of an involvement device used on a website that sells a real estate investment course. The quiz does two things: It gets prospects involved and makes them curious enough to click on a text link ("Click here for correct answer") to learn something they don't know—something that whets their appetite for the product being sold. When respondents click on the text link, a small pop-up box reveals the answer. They are *not* taken to another webpage, which poten-

W̲hat's your Real Estate IQ? Take this **simple eye-opening quiz** -- then learn **specific, cutting-edge** secrets for making **instant cash in real estate**. Answer True or False:

1. In order for you to accumulate a fortune in real estate, you need excellent credit or a lot of money.   TRUE ☐   FALSE ☐

Click here for the correct answer.

2. **Clearly,** real estate investing has created more millionaires than any other industry known to man, but it's a slow process - taking years to acquire massive wealth.   TRUE ☐   FALSE ☐

Click here for the correct answer.

3. 99.32% of today's **elite real estate millionaires** made their fortunes by buying/renting single-family homes.   TRUE ☐   FALSE ☐

Click here for the correct answer.

Figure 3.2 Questionnaire-type involvement device.

tially could take them away from the intended sales path. This is essential when designing a device like this one.

The sky's the limit when it comes to involvement devices. You're limited only by your own creativity. Figure 3.3 shows an involvement device that uses the power of commitment. Why is this powerful? According to Robert Cialdini, "Writing is believing." When you ask your readers to write down (or, in this case, to type out) the things they desire, they admit the need for your product or service. In addition, a written commitment is more lasting than a mental commitment. When you write out a commitment, you have a greater likelihood of following through than if you don't write it. Notice that I also make readers close the sale themselves by making Megabolic Weight Loss part of their commitment statement.

Now that you know that Megabolic Weight Loss is the surefire way of losing all your unwanted weight, now all that's left is for you to do what it takes to succeed. In order to do that, you need to **get leverage on yourself**.

Quite frankly, *Megabolic Weight Loss* simply cannot fail when it is implemented <u>exactly as prescribed</u>. But no weight loss program, no matter how powerful, will work if there isn't the **power of commitment** behind it.

So **type your name, the number of pounds you want to lose, and the reason/s you want to lose the weight** in the blanks below, and read the completed statement out loud to reinforce the commitment that will lead to your ultimate success:

I, _____ , have decided I want to lose ____ pounds, because _____ " and I'm committed to following the *Megabolic Weight Loss Program* until I reach my desired weight.

Figure 3.3 Involvement device that uses power of commitment.

Involvement Devices and the Recovery Principle

An involvement device I invented a few years ago makes use of the recovery principle of marketing. It not only gets people involved in the sales copy and makes them raise their hands and prequalify themselves as your target audience, but also captures their contact information. The recovery principle is not new. It's something used often in direct-response marketing.

Here's how it works: If you fail to sell your web visitors on your primary product at the full price, but succeed in selling them the same product (or perhaps a different product) at a lower unit of sale, you *recover* the effort and cost of getting viewers to your website and plug them into your income stream. That's how it got its name. Even if you don't make as much profit on each of these sales, you recover costs, which adds to your overall profitability. More important, you turn someone who might otherwise never have done business with

Before you do anything else...

... you <u>must</u> lock in your position. Even if you're not yet **100% certain** that **you're going to attend**, you can secure your position with just **your e-mail address** so that you won't lose out. <u>Don't worry that you haven't read everything yet</u> -- because you'll **pay no money** now, and you will <u>not</u> be obligated to attend the Boot Camp should you change your mind later.

When you enter your e-mail address below, you will be given a **priority reservation code** that will guarantee you **preferential** treatment over others when the limited <u>number of seats are</u> allocated.

<u>If you don't</u> lock in your position, there's a **93% chance** that you won't secure a seat -- even when you decide you want to attend. Lock in your position by entering your **e-mail address** here:

When you press GO, your entry will be **time-stamped** for preferential handling, and don't worry -- you won't be taken to another site. You'll remain right on this Web page.

Figure 3.4 Recovery involvement device.

you into a customer, and, of course, those customers have a lifetime value since they will be buying future products from you. (See Figure 3.4.)

The recovery involvement device that I used on the Guerrilla Marketing Boot Camp website accounted for almost 50 percent of the seminar attendees. Had we not installed this recovery device, we would have had only half the number of attendees. Once you understand that you don't have to offer your product at only one price, but that you can adjust your offer on the fly, you can make far greater profits than if you had not employed a recovery device, which can dramatically improve your website's profitability.

According to an *eMarketer* report, acquiring a new customer costs five to ten times more than retaining an existing one. Therefore, every effort must be made to keep customers. Some companies use the recovery approach to increase customer retention and minimize product returns. A software company sends out the following e-mail to those who want to return a product:

> Dear [name of customer],
>
> Thank you for our recent order of [name of software]. I'm sorry to hear that you've found it necessary to return the software for a refund.
>
> We've gone to great lengths to make sure that [name of software] meets the needs, and exceeds the expectations, of entrepreneurs like you. Therefore, unless you're dissatisfied with the way [name of software] performs, we'd like you to continue enjoying the benefits and convenience of owning it. In this regard, we'd like to offer you the rebate of $68.50—that's 50% of the price you

originally paid for it. We're offering you this special accommodation because we certainly don't want to lose you as a customer, and look forward to serving you for years to come.

Simply reply to this e-mail, and a check in the amount of $68.50 will be mailed to you immediately. Please understand that your acceptance of this rebate signifies your decision not to return [name of software] at some future date. Should you not wish to accept this rebate offer, and choose to return [name of software], please place it in the original packaging (or another appropriately sized box), send it back to us insured (for your protection), and we will issue a full refund of your purchase price within 4 weeks of receiving the product.

Sincerely,

[Name of customer service rep]

Marketing communications such as this one, go a long way toward retaining customers, as well as recovering the effort and cost of getting them to buy in the first place. America Online (AOL) uses a similar recovery approach when its "free trial" members call in to cancel their membership. Instead of just letting customers go without a fight, AOL offers every member wishing to cancel the opportunity to continue enjoying AOL at no charge for another month—sometimes two or more. The company is justified in thinking that if members become accustomed to using AOL, eventually they won't want to cancel.

The key to the recovery principle is that no offer has to be static. Any of its parts—the price, the duration, the warranty, the privileges—should be flexible enough to meet the needs of customers. Even if the profit margins from the downsell are considerably less than the standard margins, every unit of sale adds to the company's bottom line, helps to recover costs, and keeps customers in the company's income stream. When you consider that repeat customers spend 67 percent more—and after ten purchases, the average customer has referred seven people (Bain & Company, 2002)—every attempt to exercise the recovery principle is well worth the effort.

In my experience, I've seen website sales double or even triple with the judicious use of any *one* of the devices I've described in this chapter. This is why adding psychological and other devices is an integral part of the fleshing out process (See Chapter 2). Strategically employing these devices wherever possible in your copy is *essential* if you want to maximize the sales generated.

4

Crafting Your Copy

You can have everything in life you want if you will just help
enough other people get what they want.
—Zig Ziglar

Now that you know how to create a blueprint for writing web copy and understand how to use the five simple steps for fleshing out the body copy, including injecting psychological and involvement devices, it's time to build the house, to put your copy together and add the final important touches—the keys to making your web copy sell.

CONSTRUCTING YOUR WEB COPY

▼

The purpose of web copy—and it can't be said too often—is to generate leads, customers, sales, and consequently profits for a website. (Web copy should not be confused with web content, which is simply words written for the web for the purpose of informing, communicating, entertaining, or edifying the reader.) Web copy, therefore, is essentially another form of direct-response advertising (direct mail sales letters and TV infomercials are examples of direct-response advertising), although different media sometimes require different techniques to obtain the same results.

Direct-response advertising compels the audience to *respond* in some way or *take action* of some kind. It tells the audience to do something specific during or at the end of an ad. That response or action could be anything from calling a toll-free number for more information to sending in a coupon, visiting a store, or ordering a product.

The AIDA Principle

The four fundamentals of writing good copy are summed up in the time-honored AIDA principle:

A	Capture the audience's *attention*.
I	Get the audience's *interest*.

D   Build *desire* (for your offer).

A   Induce *action.*

Benefits and Features.   Features are the attributes, properties, or characteristics of your product or service. Benefits, on the other hand, are what you can *do,* what you can *have,* or what you can *be* because of those features. People buy benefits—*not* features. This is one of the most important lessons you can learn in writing copy. For example, people don't buy a power drill for its impressive specs; rather, they buy the holes that the power drill makes.

When writing copy that sells, therefore, you want to keep your eye firmly on the benefits. The best way to distinguish benefits from features is with the following exercise: Begin by stating the feature. Then follow it up with the sentence, "What that means to you is . . ." or the phrase, ". . . which means that you can . . ."

Feature: Intel's new microprocessor for mobile PCs has a speed of 2 gigahertz.

Benefit: *which means that* you can *play online games wherever you go.*

Feature: The Mobile Intel Pentium 4 Processor-M laptop is a 2-GHz system.

Benefit: *what that means to you is,* you can *take it with you* on your summer vacations and road trips so you can *listen* to MP3 music files, *entertain the kids* with DVD movies, *store* your digital *photographs,* and *stay connected* with family and friends via e-mail.

The Unique Selling Proposition

One of the cornerstones of writing sales-pulling copy is the unique selling proposition (USP), the thing that sets you, your product/service, or your business apart from every other competitor in a *favorable* way. It's the *competitive advantage* that you proclaim to your prospects, customers, or clients.

Three of the best-known USPs are these:

> Avis Rent A Car: *"We're number two. We try harder."*
>
> FedEx: *"When it absolutely, positively has to get there overnight."*
>
> Domino's Pizza: *"Fresh, hot pizza in 30 minutes or less."*

More than just slogans, these USPs convey the idea that no other company, product, or service compares with theirs.

Amazon.com proclaims itself "Earth's Biggest Bookstore," a claim that has been accepted without question by the media, both online and offline. Its USP implies that it has the best selection of books; in essence, "if you can't find it here, you can't find it anywhere," thereby distinguishing Amazon from all other bookstores. Although Amazon.com is indeed the largest *online-only bookstore* in the world, Barnes & Noble is "the world's largest bookseller," if you include both on- and offline markets. Amazon.com has managed to blur that distinction by achieving *top-of-mind positioning* with its USP.

A USP positions your offering as being different from, and consequently *more valuable than,* your competitors' offering. It distinguishes your product or service from everyone else's, and in a world that's flooded with products and services of every kind, creating a strong USP is absolutely imperative. It gives your reader a *specific* and *compelling* reason to buy from you instead of your competitors. It not only establishes the direction of copywriting, but is the undercurrent of all marketing efforts as well.

There are online companies whose USP is clearly conveyed by their domain name. Lowestfare.com (which claims to provide the lowest airfares in the air travel industry) and Internet-AudioMadeEasy.com (which claims to enable people to easily add streaming audio to their websites) are examples of these. Their names say it all.

One way to develop a USP is by starting with the words, "Unlike most of its competitors . . . ," then filling in the blanks about what differentiates you or your product offering from those of others. For example,

Unlike most other fat-burning products, ABC Product makes you lose up to 5 pounds of pure body fat per week—without the use of stimulants that may be harmful to your health.

Another way to develop a USP is to highlight a feature or benefit that *only* your product or service contains or features.

Serious Magic, a software company, sells a product called Visual Communicator. Its USP is that it enables people with no technical experience to create with ease—in minutes and without any video editing—video presentations for websites, DVDs, and PowerPoint that have the professional look of a TV newscast. The specificity of the USP ("people with no technical experience," "professional look of a TV newscast in minutes," and "without any video editing") is compelling and serves to differentiate the product from other programs offering video creation capabilities.

The possibilities for crafting a USP are endless. The key is to adopt a USP that fills a void in the marketplace that you or your product can genuinely fill. Remember, too, that a USP can even be used as a headline or as an underlying theme or branding mechanism for all copywriting.

MAKING AN IMPRESSION: THE FIRST PARAGRAPH

The first paragraph is crucial because it is where readers are likely to stop reading if you don't provide them with sufficient reason to continue. Ideally, it should immediately demonstrate that there are desirable rewards for reading on.

There's no need to be lengthy or elaborate. Often, short, punchy, easy-to-read sentences suffice as long as they hold the viewer's attention. One device that some leading copywriters use is to ask a question that will grip the readers' interest and compel them to continue reading.

THE OFFER YOU CAN'T REFUSE ▼

The offer is the very heart of your copy. It is the reason the copy is being written. When writing copy for offline consumption, once you have captured the attention of your readers you need to present your offer as soon as possible to let them know what you are selling and what kind of deal you'll be making. When writing web copy for direct-response offers, that's not necessarily the case. Particularly when writing editorial-style web copy, you must be careful not to uncover your hidden selling too soon. If you do, you will remove all doubt that your editorial is actually an ad in disguise.

Whether you are writing copy for on- or offline use, your offer needs to be *clear, concise,* and above all *irresistible.* For example:

> Own this deluxe set of knives that never need sharpening for just $19.95—and you'll never buy another set of knives again. It comes with a lifetime replacement guarantee. In the unlikely event that any of these knives should break—we will replace any or all of them free of charge—forever.

Your offer must align with your target audience's desires and needs and, as you know, must appeal to their emotions.

What motivates people to buy? Steven Reiss, a professor of psychology and psychiatry at Ohio State University, in his book *Who Am I? The 16 Basic Desires That Motivate Our Action and*

Define Our Personalities, describes his theory of human motivation. Reiss, who spent five years conducting studies involving 6,000 people, discovered that these 16 desires—power, independence, curiosity, acceptance, order, saving, honor, idealism, social contact, family, status, vengeance, romance, eating, physical exercise, and tranquility—motivate all human behavior. Other studies add the desire to belong, security, integrity, consistency, ownership, exclusivity, safety, admiration, and acknowledgment. All of these complex human desires can be grouped into two basic human needs: the desire to *gain pleasure* and *avoid pain.*

Since copywriting ultimately is about fulfilling human desires and needs, the more successful you are at representing your product or service in a way that plays to those desires and needs, the more successful your sales copy will be. When articulating the offer, your primary viewpoint should always be that of your reader. In other words, you need to *focus entirely on your reader.* One of the best ways to pull your reader into your copy is by weaving the words *you, your,* or *yourself* throughout. This gets your readers involved in what you are saying and makes them feel as though you are writing to them.

Your offer must summarize the key benefits and advantages of the product or service you're selling. This is effectively done through bullet points—to make the copy more readable and inviting. Following are examples of bullet points for a software program aimed at novel writers:

▶ Walks you, step-by-step, through the process of writing your story—it's like having a personal writing mentor and tutor interactively showing you how to write a great novel.

- ▶ Simplifies the process of developing a solidly con-structed plot and outline for your novel—the plot gen-erator gives you instant access to thousands of suggested plots from virtually all kinds of stories.

- ▶ Enables you to create rich, dynamic characters with the easy-to-use character developer.

- ▶ Allows you to instantly find answers to specific ques-tions, and get targeted advice for resolving problems while you write.

- ▶ Provides suggestions to over 100 stumbling blocks that frequently face beginning novelists.

- ▶ Includes a troubleshooter function that takes you from your writing problem to its remedy with a click of the mouse.

TESTIMONIALS: IT *CAN* HAPPEN TO YOU

▼

Testimonials add *credibility* because they are the actual words of real people, *not* actors or spokespeople. They can be quite dis-arming because your readers are able to identify with other people's experiences with your product or service.

You can obtain testimonials by simply asking for them when you fulfill orders, or by calling or e-mailing customers and asking for their comments. What was their experience with your product or service: Did they enjoy it? Are they glad they purchased it? When you get positive comments, ask permission to use them in your ad, and don't forget to get a signed release.

The best testimonials are the ones that are *specific* and, preferably, *quantifiable*.

> With the ABC product, I lost 10 pounds in 9 days without dieting.

> I earned 5 times my salary in my spare time by following the ABC system.

TALKING ABOUT MONEY: HOW TO INTRODUCE THE PRICE

▼

First and most important, you must *never* introduce the price until you've stated the offer. If you do, the majority of your readers might click away before ever learning the more salient points of your offer. Second, when you do introduce the price, equate it with a ridiculously minor purchase, or reduce it to a daily cost.

Minor-Purchase Technique

Here's how the minor-purchase technique was used to introduce the price of a book about how to write news releases:

> Bottom line is, for a few bucks more than the price of a movie for two (with popcorn), you can get your hands on the secrets that would mean truckloads of hot leads,

sales that would make your head spin, a surge of cash flowing into your business, and first-rate recognition for you and your product that money just can't buy.

Daily-Cost Technique

Here's how the price was introduced for a shopping cart service that costs $29 per month:

For just $1 a day, you can now automate your . . .

- ► order processing
- ► e-mail marketing
- ► ad tracking
- ► credit card processing
- ► recurring billing
- ► affiliate program
- ► the digital delivery of your electronic products

. . . and all other e-commerce activities your website requires.

This tactic, known as *equating* also can be used when you are conveying a time frame in your web copy. For example, "In the time it takes you to brew a cup of coffee, you're done with your marketing for the day."

❑ Yes! I want the *Promotional Products Distributorship Program* delivered to me immediately, and to learn how to grab my share of the $18 billion promotional products industry in as little as 1 week. I understand that I will also receive the following bonuses worth $1300!

· A $100 discount off the regular $995 price of the Distributorship Program. *(Therefore, my price is only $895.)*

· A 15-minute telephone consultation with Joe McVoy personally (an $87.50 value)—absolutely FREE—to help me get off to a great start in the industry

· Unlimited e-mail consultation for 2 full months (60 days). ($350 value)

· Annual directory updates—FREE promotional product manufacturer directories ($770 value)

· A FREE copy of *Promotional Marketing* Magazine, a valuable resource of product information for distributors. Plus information on how to get this magazine sent to you automatically every month at absolutely no charge.

I understand that my order is absolutely risk-free. If, after one year, I have not earned at least 5 times my investment—that is, $4,475—by implementing any of the powerful money-making tactics found in the Distributor Program, I can return it for a 100% refund.

I authorize Promotional Products Consulting, LLC to charge my credit card the amount of $895.00 (+ applicable shipping charges; UPS Ground is only $47.25, UPS 2nd Day is $127.00. Alaska/Hawaii 2nd Day is $139.50).

Here's what Joe Ferraro of Universal Showdown Marketing says: "I've had a screenprinting business for 10 years. I added a promotional products profit center to my business by simply following exactly what Joe McVoy taught me to do in his Distributor Program—which had all the factory sources I needed. In only 7 months, I've started earning a 6-figure income. I've decided to close down my screenprinting business to concentrate on my lucrative promotional products business full-time."

Click here to proceed to the secure order form.

Figure 4.1

KEEP ON SELLING: WRITING THE ORDER FORM

▼

When I worked as director for creative web writing at Aesop Marketing Corporation, Mark Joyner designed an order form that increased orders by more than 30 percent. Ever since Mark revealed this information in his report, *Confidential Internet Intelligence Manuscript,* it's been used successfully by online marketers all over the world. I often use the proven format shown in Figure 4.1.

The order form features the following components:

- ► Check box—an involvement device that compels prospects to agree to the sale the moment they click on the check box

- ► Summary of offer, bonuses, and guarantee

- ► Price

- ► Assurance of secure ordering

- ► How the product or service will be delivered—and when

- ► Testimonial as reinforcement of purchase

THE MONEY-BACK GUARANTEE: A DEAL MAKER
▼

Frequently, the sale is clinched on the promise of a money-back guarantee. This is where you *eliminate* the buyer risk, thus removing any remaining obstacles standing in the way the sale.

Simply stating "Money-back guarantee" is an ineffective use of a guarantee, however. You have to craft the guarantee as compellingly as possible so as not to waste this prime opportunity for closing the sale. A common template for creating a guarantee is as follows:

Do this [*whatever you're asking them to do*], and if you don't [*achieve the result you're claiming they'll get*], then simply give us a call, and we will cheerfully refund your entire purchase price.

For example,

> Take the ABC system for a test drive. If you don't triple your sales in 60 days, then return it for a full refund.

By removing the risk, you make it easier for the prospect to say yes. It is a well-documented fact in direct marketing that the number of people who will take you up on a compelling offer significantly outnumber those who will ask for a refund.

> **Try the Memory Foam mattress pad *now*, risk-free.** If it doesn't give you the most restful sleep you've ever had, or if, for any reason, you're not completely satisfied with it, just let us know within 30 days and we will issue a no-hassle refund, and even send you a Merchandise Return Label so that you can send the mattress pad back to us at no cost to you—we'll pay for the shipping. In the unlikely event that you would be less than **thrilled** with your new Memory Foam mattress pad, should you decide to request a refund, the 2 Memory Foam pillows are yours to keep and enjoy as our gift just for taking us up on this offer.

A strong guarantee conveys *conviction*, which has the power to *persuade* your prospect. It is sometimes possible to construct a guarantee that is so compelling that it could be *the reason* why someone chooses your product or service over your competitors'. In fact, your guarantee could be so powerful that you might also consider using it as your headline:

Drive This New Pontiac for 30 Days—and If It's Not the Greatest Car You've Ever Had, We'll Buy It Back

Drop 5 Strokes on Your Golf Game Today—*Guaranteed*

THE CLOSE: SIGNING ON THE DOTTED LINE ▼

Legendary marketer and copywriter Vic Schwab, who authored the classic "*How to Write a Good Advertisement: A Short Course in Copywriting,*" said, "Delay is the enemy of a sale." In writing web copy, your close needs to remove all obstacles that stand in the way of the reader taking action on the offer. The way to do it is by first making the offer and then injecting a sense of *urgency* in taking action on the offer.

Injecting urgency simply means giving the reader a reason to act now. You can employ one or more of the following:

▶ A free gift/bonus or a discount or reduced price *if* the reader responds on or before a certain date in the near future. Sweeten the deal, and whet the appetite. Sometimes the bonus can be so compelling that, like the guarantee, it can even be the headline.

▶ A time limit on an offer.

▶ A limited supply.

▶ A notification that prices are going up soon.

The close should also emphasize what the reader gains by responding quickly or loses by delaying action.

Call to Action

The *call to action* (CTA) is part of the close. Here, you must tell your reader *exactly* what to do. Some marketers miss this important step. Even if it's obvious to you what the reader ought to do next, you must *direct* them to do it. Always use action verbs in the CTA:

Click on the Download button to start your 30-day free trial.

Check the box to select your preference, and then click on *secure online form* to proceed with your order.

Simply type your name and e-mail address in the form below, and the free report will be in your e-mail box within minutes.

Click on the link below to start generating eBay profits now.

Type in your e-mail address, then click on Go to lock in your position.

GET A CALLING CARD: THE OPT-IN MECHANISM

▼

We all know that most visitors to websites don't become buyers on their first visit. Maybe not even on the first several visits. What you want to do is find out how to reach them again.

The best way to do this is with an opt-in mechanism (a tool to get a reader to agree to accept your e-mailed information and correspondence). Remember, the odds are against people buying something the first time they visit your website. After all, they don't even know you. Therefore, you must develop an irresistible—and easy—way for your visitors, at minimum, to give you their e-mail address before they go.

In my opinion, crafting your opt-in offer is infinitely more important than crafting the offer for the product itself. That's because you can get as much as 90 percent of your business from those with whom you build an e-mail relationship. This is the usual objective, but I advise you not to be shortsighted and focus only on selling, but also on building relationships.

HOW TO CONSTRUCT A RIVETING HEADLINE

According to David Ogilvy, founder of the Ogilvy & Mather advertising agency and author of *Confessions of an Advertising Man* and *Ogilvy on Advertising,* "On the average, *five times* as many people *read the headlines* as read the body copy. It follows that, unless your headline sells your product, you have wasted 90 percent of your money."

Here's a plan for crafting never-fail headlines:

Step 1. Write 30 to 50 headlines before you decide on the one you're going to use.

Step 2. Step back from the headline for a day and read it again with a fresh perspective.

Step 3. Ask yourself, "How can this headline be better?" "Is this the best possible headline for my objective, my target audience, and my product or service?"

Most important, *don't* take shortcuts when crafting the headline. If you write a weak one, you will have failed, because no matter how good the rest of the piece is, no one will ever read it, and, consequently, no one will buy what you're selling. Remember, the most important element of a website is the first screen, and the most important element of the first screen is the headline. Therefore, you must give it the attention it deserves.

The headline (or opening statement or its equivalent) is the most important component of any direct-response ad, whether it's a printed sales letter or an "advertorial" on your web site. If you don't stop readers dead in their tracks with your headline, you don't stand a chance of making a sale.

The sales-producing ability of your website is directly proportional to the number of people who read what's on it. That is, the more people who read your web copy, the more sales it will generate. Therefore, the headline must grab the reader's attention, since its primary purpose is to induce people to start reading the copy.

John Caples (the advertising industry's advocate of rigorously tested, measured, and verifiable advertising effectiveness) said in his book, *Tested Advertising Methods,* "In a print ad, 75 percent of the buying decisions are made at the headline alone." I'm speculating that online, that percentage might be a bit less—perhaps 60 to 65 percent. Although I haven't found statistics to support my contention, after factoring in the attention deficit, information overwhelm, and general skepticism so prevalent on the web, I feel reasonably comfortable with my speculation; 60 to 65 percent is still significant enough that you should take the subject of headlines more seriously than any other aspect of web copy.

What's in a Headline?

Your headline should convey a benefit of interest to your target audience. It must answer the reader's unspoken question, "What's in it for me?" As we've learned, there are two basic approaches to answering that question, and each stems from one of two basic human needs: (1) to gain pleasure or (2) to avoid pain.

You can appeal to the human need to gain pleasure by pointing out how the readers can attain or accomplish something—or gain, save, take advantage, or profit—by using your product or service. More particularly, your headline can demonstrate how your product or service will meet your readers' needs or solve their problems. Here are some classic examples of headlines with appeals based on pleasure:

The Secret to Making People Like You

How I Sold $200 Million Worth of Products and Services

Make Anyone Do Anything You Mentally Command—
With Your Mind Alone!

How to Win Friends and Influence People

Why Some Consultants Earn $100,000 to $250,000 per
Year While Most Struggle Just to Get By

Play Guitar in Seven Days or Your Money Back

Alternatively, you can appeal to the human need to avoid pain by showing how readers can reduce or eliminate undesirable things such as discomfort, embarrassment, loss, illness, mistakes, poverty, or boredom, to name a few. Here are a few famous ones that play on that need:

Do You Make These Mistakes in English?

Are You Ever Tongue-Tied at a Party?

You Can Laugh at Money Worries—If You Follow This Simple Plan

When Doctors Feel "Rotten," This Is What They Do

Do You Have These Symptoms of Nerve Exhaustion?

Do You Do Any of These 10 Embarrassing Things?

All of these successful headlines are compelling. They not only capture the attention of prospective buyers, they also make an immediate connection with them. They give the reader a good reason to read on.

The Building Blocks of Winning Web Headlines

Headlines are the starting point of successful web copy. If your headline fails to capture the attention of the reader, it doesn't matter how good your body copy is because your reader won't ever get there. According to master direct marketer and author Ted Nicholas, who reportedly has sold $500 million worth of products in 49 industries, a good headline can be as much as 17 times more effective than a so-so headline. Simply changing one word or one figure in a headline can dramatically improve the response.

A successful headline engages or involves the reader by

- ► Offering a strong, compelling promise

    Open Your Own Personally Branded, Fully Stocked Online Store in 15 Minutes

- ► Highlighting benefits to the reader

    The World's Richest Source of Cash—And How You Can Tap into It to Start or Grow Your Business"

- ► Explaining exactly what the offer is;

    Earn Your Master's Degree Online in 18 Months or Less

- ► Appealing to the emotions

    Will These Internet Trends Kill Your Online Business?

- ► Using specifics

    How Adam Ginsberg Made $15 Million on eBay in 2003

- ► Arousing curiosity

    Words That Command People to Do Your Bidding

- ► Calling out to a specific target audience

    The Sales-Closing Techniques of a Self-Made Billionaire

- ► Making an announcement

    $2 Million Scientific Project Unlocks the Secret of Aging: How You Can Become Biologically Younger

> ▶ Asking a question
>
>> Does Coral Calcium Really Reverse Aging, Extend Your Life Span, and Cure Degenerative Diseases Like Cancer?
>
> ▶ Beginning with the words *how to*
>
>> How to Control the Mind of Your Prospects—And Influence Them to Buy What You're Selling

Building Block 1. Web headlines differ from advertising headlines because a web headline doesn't always explain what the offer is. Instead, it wraps the offer in an editorial cushion. Like the body copy, the headline should not read like an ad; rather it should read like an editorial. Remember, according to Ted Nicholas, five times as many people read editorials than messages that scream out, "I'm an ad!" If an advertorial is prepared in a way that lends credibility, it can pull up to 500 percent more in sales!

Building Block 2. When writing a headline that highlights benefits, remember that there are obvious benefits as well as hidden ones. An obvious benefit is one that is immediately apparent. Even then, the obvious must be articulated in a way that conveys value. For example, say you are trying to convey the money-saving benefit of joining a buyers discount club. Instead of writing a bland headline like "Save 20 Percent on All Your Purchases," I'd write the following:

Discover How to Give Yourself a 20 Percent Pay Raise—
Without Having to Squeeze a Single Cent from Your Boss

Do you see the hidden benefit? When you save 20 percent or more on everything you buy (as a discount buying club member), that's the equivalent of getting a 20 percent pay raise (and you don't have to pay taxes on that pay raise!). I've stated the obvious in a creative way, and added emotion and drama into it by using the action words, *discover* and *squeeze.*

A hidden benefit is one that is not immediately apparent and, at first glance, may not seem to be a reason for buying your product or service. "A Tax-Deductible Vacation in Las Vegas" is a hidden benefit of attending a seminar in Las Vegas.

Building Block 3.   According to master copywriter and marketer Ted Nicholas, who reportedly spent more than $100,000 testing to find out which copy elements boost response rates, an ad headline draws 28 percent more attention if framed in quotation marks! The ad appears much more important because the impression that someone is being quoted adds credibility, which in turn makes it more riveting and more likely to be read. For example, "You, Too, Can Pick Winning Stocks—with 95 Percent Accuracy."

Building Block 4.   Whenever possible, use the imperative voice in your headline. The imperative voice is a grammatical mood that (as its name implies) influences the behavior of another or expresses a command.

Land a Better Job

Put an End to Migraines

Erase Your Negative Credit Marks

Cancel Your Debts

Stop the Flu Dead in Its Tracks

The imperative voice commands, leads or empowers your prospect to do something. It starts with an action verb (such as *blast, impress, improve, create*); it assumes the subject is *you* and ends with the object of the action. If your verb is *blast*, the question is, blast what? And the answer is, *your competition*. The headline is: Blast Your Competition. If your action verb is *impress*, the question is, impress whom? Answer, *your friends*. The headline is: Impress Your Friends.

CHOOSING YOUR WORDS: TIPS, TERMS, AND CONCEPTS
▼

Once you've written your copy, it is vital that you pay attention to how *readable* that copy is. Short sentences and simple words make your copy more inviting. They also help to cut up huge blocks of text into bite-size paragraphs that are no more than three or four sentences each.

Microsoft Word has a tool that displays information about the reading level of the document, including readability scores. It rates text on a 100-point scale; the higher the score, the easier it is for people to understand your writing. Aim for a score of 70 or higher. It also rates your writing on a U.S. grade-school level. For example, a score of 7.0 means that a seventh grader can understand the document. When writing copy, aim for a score of seventh- or eighth-grade-level comprehension.

Words to Avoid in Your Web Copy

You already know that you should avoid using intellectual, rational, or right-brained words, opting instead for emotional words, but there are other categories of words you must avoid using.

Don't use euphemisms (more agreeable or more politically correct words and expressions) in an effort to avoid words that may offend or suggest something unpleasant. Doing so will insult the intelligence of your audience. While you think you are trying to spare your readers' feelings and sensibilities, using euphemisms may backfire and cause readers to be more offended than if you had just been straightforward. For example, don't call overweight people "metabolically challenged" or people who suffer from hair loss "follicularly challenged" or poor people "economic underachievers." People see through these euphemisms and may think you are actually condescending.

Don't use buzzwords (important-sounding words or phrases used primarily to impress laypersons) if the buzzwords don't play an integral part in your selling proposition. In other words, don't use buzzwords just to show people that you're cool, that you're hip to modern lingo, or to impress them with your vocabulary. Some examples currently in use include *proactive, downsizing, supersize, outsourcing, actionable,* and *impact* used as a verb (as in "impact your business").

Buzzwords sometimes alienate people who don't understand what you are talking about. They may also make you sound pompous or pretentious. Even worse, you may be using words that have gone hopelessly out of style (without your knowing it), which makes you appear *so* twentieth century.

Don't use corporatespeak. The way you write web copy is distinctly different from the way you would write a corporate communication or even a literary or journalistic work. As I tell my students, "You're not going to win any literary awards for writing excellent web copy, but you are going to win sales." You may pride yourself on writing flowery prose or businesslike correspondence, but those things don't cut it in web copy. For instance, the words, "We are committed to your success," don't mean anything to people anymore. It's tired, it's boring, and it doesn't convey tangible benefits.

Don't use clichés. I believe the avoidance of clichés applies to all genres of writing. They diminish the value of your writing. Clichés make your writing look terribly dated, which in turn may affect how your readers view your offer. If you are behind the times, what does that say about your product or service?

Don't use tentative adjectives. These are words like *pretty* as in "pretty good," *very* as in "very impressive," or *quite* as in "quite wonderful." Such words rob your writing of conviction. You must either drop the word altogether and simplify your sentence, or replace the word with a compelling one that dramatizes the thought you are trying to communicate.

Do communicate. We've all heard the Internet referred to as the information superhighway. In fact, it's practically a cliché. But information is distinctly different from *communication*. The Internet is filled with people who can inundate you with all kinds of information; the person who has the ability to communicate is the one who will rise above the clutter and the noise—and actually be heard or read.

Author Sidney J. Harris once said, "The two words 'information' and 'communication' are often used interchangeably, but they signify quite different things. Information is giving out; communication is getting through." In marketing, you want to use words that communicate, words that will create interest, trigger enthusiasm, and motivate people to action. Words that will "get through."

WORDS TO USE IN YOUR WEB COPY ▼

Here are some eye-catching words that create positive or engaging images.

Attention-Grabbing Words

Affordable	Challenging
Alert	Competitive edge
Allure	Comprehensive
Applause	Compromise
Avoiding	Concept
	Crucial
Big	
Billboard	Daring
Block busting	Danger
Bonanza	Destiny
Boom	Dirty
Bottom line	Distinguished
Brain picking	Dividends
Bravo	Dynamics
Breakthrough	
Buy	Eager
Buyer's guide	Easy

Eat	Giant
Economic needs	Good-looking
Effective	Growth
Emerging growth	Gut feelings
Endurance	
Energy	Happy
Enterprising	Heritage
Envision	High tech
Epidemic	High yield
Excitement	Hit
Exercising	Hopeless
Expert	Hot property
Explain	Hybrid
Exploit	Hurry
Favorable	Idea
Find out	Imagination
Flex	Inflation-beating
Flourishes	Innovative
Focus	Investigative
Foothold	Insatiable
Forecast	
Formula	Just in time
Fueling	
Fundamentals	Keep in touch
Funny	Kidding
Gaining	Last-minute
Gallery	Late-breaking
Generic	Launching
Get	Liberated

Lifeblood

Lively

Longevity

Lucky

Luxury

Mainstream

Make

Mania

Marvelous

Masterpiece

Measure up

Medicine

Merit

Monitor

Monumental

Naked

Nest egg

New

Newswire

Next frontier

Nostalgic

Novel

Obsession

Opportunities

Overrated

Perspective

Philosophy

Pioneering

Portfolio

Preppie

Profitable decision

Promising

Recruiting

Remarkable

Reminiscent

Renaissance spirit

Reviewing

Revisited

Revolution

Rewards

Rich

Right now

Sampler

Save

Savvy

School of thought

Scorecard

Security

Show me

Shrewd

Simplistic

Skill

Slash

Smart

Spiral

Soar

Specialized	Test-drive
Speed up	Timely
Spotlight	Top dog
Stardom	Traces
Starter kit	
Stop	Ultimate
Stubborn	Underpriced
Successful switch	Unlock
Surefire	Upscale
Surging	
Survival	Value line
Tax-resistant	Willpower
Tech revolution	Word-of-mouth
Technology	
Tell	Young

DOs AND DON'Ts OF WEB COPYWRITING ▼

Do give a compelling promise early in the body copy that the material viewers are about to read is worth their while. For example:

> Be sure to *read every word* of this because the secret ingredient for turning your small business enterprise into a mega-success story is hidden in this article.

In the next example, I challenge them to read every word, because if they don't, they'll miss that thing they are dying to know.

Your first step is to *read this article in its entirety*. Please don't just skim through it—I don't want you to miss a single word, because when I demystify web copywriting for you, you simply cannot fail to create the sales and profits you want on the web.

Another technique I use is to reveal a little-known fact, anecdote, or case study at the beginning, followed by a statement like this:

If you think that's interesting, wait 'til you read what I've discovered.

This statement implies that more interesting information is about to be revealed. In the next example, the promise of "solid proof" is compelling, and makes readers continue reading with anticipation.

The career of writing no longer has to be synonymous with "starving." An annual income of $100,000 or more—even on a freelance or part-time basis—is now well within your reach. This is absolutely no hype—and I'll give you *solid proof* in a moment. And if you think that's exciting, wait 'til I show you how you can do it in as little as 6 weeks.

This is how it works when you put it all together: In your introductory paragraphs, tell your readers what you are going to say with a compelling promise. In the body copy, deliver on the promise, and, in a concluding paragraph, remind them of what you just revealed. This boosts your credibility for delivering on a promise and paves the way toward making your reader welcome your offer.

Do establish early in the copy who is writing the piece and why the audience should believe the writer. This is where your (or your client's) credentials, qualifications, or experience become important. They don't necessarily have to be monumental; that is, you don't have to be the leading expert or authority in a particular field, but your credentials must make you (or your client) believable.

One *html trick* I use to identify the writer (i.e., the person in whose "voice" the web copy is expressed) early in the piece is to make the writer's name a *hypertext link*. When visitors click on the link, it opens a pop-up window containing the qualifications of the writer.

Do write in the first person. Whenever possible, remove the words *we* or *our* from your web copy and replace them with *I*. By speaking in the first person, it is as though one person is talking to another. *We* and *our* sound more corporate, less intimate and friendly. You can't use this technique all of the time, but do use it when it's appropriate.

Do use a *drop letter* (also called a *drop cap*) when starting your body copy. A drop letter is an *oversized* (often bold and ornamental) first letter of the first sentence of your body copy. Generally, it drops down two or more lines into the opening text of your body copy. Tests conducted by Ted Nichols have proven that starting your body copy with a drop cap increases readership because it draws readers' eyes to it, thereby leading them to start reading the body copy instead of clicking away.

Do use multiple pricing structures. Always remember that people fall into different price categories. That's why Mercedes-Benz makes cars that cost $27,000, $69,000, $85,000, or more.

Most people fail to recognize this when they design their offers. As a result, their offers are static. They usually have just one price and one offer.

Different pricing programs are structured to catch as many people as possible at the buying level at which they are willing to buy. Remember: The value of any merchandise is what someone is willing to pay for it.

People also gravitate to different income promises: If you run a headline that reads, "How to Use Website Metrics to Boost Your Conversion Rates to 10%, 20%—Even 30%," you're likely to get more responses than if your headline reads, "How to Use Website Metrics to Boost Your Conversion Rate to 30%." Why? Because a broader spectrum of the audience can relate to—and believe—the three levels of improvement (10, 20, and 30 percent). Some people would have trouble believing anyone could get a 30 percent conversion rate, but might readily believe that 10 or 20 percent is possible.

Remember that when you write web copy. Say I write the following headline to promote a web copywriting course: "Earn $300 Per Hour as a Web Copywriter." Very few people would read any further. The claim sounds unbelievable, even though it's true. Some people think it's not possible for them to earn that much. If, on the other hand, I write, "Can You Really Earn $85, $125—even $235 an Hour as a Web Copywriter?" and a subheadline that reads, "The Web Price Index Says You Can," that would make more people read on, wouldn't it?

Do call attention to the flaws or shortcomings of your product or service, but *only* if you can turn those flaws and shortcomings into *benefits*. When you admit the drawbacks of your product or service, you immediately increase your credibility. People think you are really up front and honest about the not-so-great aspects of your product, not just touting the good things about it. The key here is that you should not call attention to flaws or drawbacks unless you can turn that "confession" into a benefit. Avis said it this way: "We're Number 2. We try harder," and turned a drawback into a unique selling proposition. I'm sure you've often heard this said: "We're not cheap, but we're the best."

Do ask an opening question. I have already discussed the importance of incorporating compelling questions in your web copy to grab the attention of your readers and to force their brains to answer the questions more imaginatively than you can articulate them. When you open the first paragraph of your web copy with a question, it increases your chances of getting your readers to read on.

A well-designed question will cause the prospect's thoughts to focus on what you have to say. Your opening question must, of course, be relevant and important and must speak to the needs of your audience. When crafted skillfully, questions point to the result or benefit of your product or service.

Do craft text links that are engaging and highly clickable. We already know that web visitors often scan the page instead of reading it word for word. When they do, their eyes gravitate to formatting devices such as words in bold print or italics, underlined words, bullets, and the like. Text links or hyperlinks are also formatting devices.

Text links are those colored, underlined words that, when clicked on, send readers to a predetermined location in the same document, or to another webpage or website. These are even more eye-catching than bold, underlined, or italicized words because they're in another color.

It takes more than a vague "click here" to compel readers to click through to the target destination. In order for the text link to be highly clickable, it must either convey a benefit or employ an embedded command.

Click here to *find your million-dollar domain name.*

Notice that this example contains an embedded command, conveys a benefit, is written in the imperative voice (starts with an action verb, assumes the subject *you,* and ends with the object of the action). These kinds of text links are significantly more clickable. "Give it a try, risk-free" as a clickable link is more effective than "Click here to order."

Do use phrases that take the edge off the act of purchasing and make it look easy (painless) and that, ideally, convey a benefit:

Submit Your Online Reservation

Unlock the Cash Vault Now

Click Here to Get Your Name in the News

Become an Associate

Get [product] now

Attend the Boot Camp

This enhances the editorial approach to writing web copy. If you can avoid using words like "buy now" or "order" inside your editorial web copy, do it.

THE LONG AND SHORT OF IT: HOW LONG SHOULD WEB COPY BE? ▼

I'm often asked if web copy has to consist of multiple pages in order to sell—especially since most people don't read on the web. While there will always be companies, products, and services for which abbreviated web copy is both suitable and adequate, I believe that when you're trying to convince people to invest any amount of money or time (or both), you need to assure them that they are making the right purchase decision.

Most often, you simply can't do that in a single page or less of copy. That would be like expecting a customer to walk into Circuit City and walk out five minutes later with a brand-new printer after spending 60 seconds with a salesperson pitching that particular brand. That's just not how buying decisions are made, and that's just not the anatomy of the sales process.

How long should web copy be? My answer used to be this: "Web copy should be like the length of a woman's skirt—long enough to cover the subject, but short enough to be interesting." Although that answer may sound clever, and does hold seeds of truth, a more accurate reply is, "Web copy should be as long as it takes to make the sale. Period."

This policy holds true in offline copywriting as well. In his book, *Ogilvy on Advertising,* David Ogilvy wrote: "All my experience says that for a great many products, long copy sells more than short. . . . Direct response advertisers know that short copy doesn't sell. In split run tests, long copy invariably outsells short copy."

In his first Rolls-Royce advertisement, Ogilvy used 719 words, and he found that the advertisement was thoroughly read. Spurred on by the success of long copy in garnering attention, he used 1,400 words in his second Rolls-Royce advertisement, also with excellent results.

Another well-known example demonstrating the effectiveness of long copy is the Schlitz beer advertisement written by legendary copywriter, Claude Hopkins. Hopkins wrote five pages of text, and, as a result of that campaign, Schlitz moved up from fifth place to first in beer sales.

Never have I seen a high-ticket item sold in less than several pages of copy—either online or offline. As a rule, the higher the price of what you are selling, the longer the web copy should be. For example, the web copy I wrote for Jay Conrad Levinson's Guerrilla Marketing Boot Camp took 13 pages to make a $2,500 sale. But when you consider that those hardworking 13 pages sold more than half a million dollars' worth of seminar seats, you begin to understand the value of long copy.

When you learn the principles of writing long direct-response web copy, you will be able to write short web copy easily. It's similar to going to medical school and specializing in surgery. If you were a brain surgeon who later decided to become a general practitioner, you could do that.

However, the length is *not* always dependent on the price of the product or service you are selling. For example, the web copy I wrote to sell an e-class with a ticket price of $1,500 was only six pages long, while the web copy I wrote for a $27 book took all of eight pages. Both sold very well. It all points back to writing web copy that's as long or as short as it takes to make the sale.

The more practice you have writing web copy, the better feel you will have for the rhythm of the sale and the sentiments of your audience, and you'll know instinctively how long or short your web copy needs to be. The warp-speed copywriting exercise in Chapter 1 will fine-tune your instincts.

Of course, there is also such a thing as web copy that is too long. I've seen a 75-page sales letter used on a website to promote an Internet marketing seminar. There may be people who will read something that long, but generally speaking, that length will overwhelm most people. Above all, don't use long copy as an excuse to babble on and on. Your web copy needs to be a lean, mean selling machine, even if it is disguised as editorial content. It pays to remember what advertising master John Caples once said about the length of copy: "It can't be too long, only too boring."

HOW WELL DOES YOUR WEBSITE SELL? ▼

In the years I've spent specializing in web copywriting, I've developed a comprehensive formula for mathematically measuring the selling quotient of web copy. I coined the term *selling quotient* (SQ), which is the predictor of a website's sales performance based on its web copy.

You can plug this formula into your existing web copy and determine exactly what kind of a selling job your website is doing. You can also use it as a tool for evaluating web copy that you have written following the guidelines in the first four chapters of this book.

This formula allows you to grade your web copy on a scale of 1 to 100. The real beauty in the formula, though, is that even if your website scores low, you will know exactly how to fix it.

Formula for Mathematically Measuring the Selling Quotient of Web Copy

Rate the following components of your website, giving yourself a possible score of 100 points.

First Screen

Does the first screen give the web visitor a compelling reason—in 5 seconds or less—why he or she should stay and read on? (0–7)   _____

Note: Did you make sure that the logo, company name, header, graphics, and other nonselling features did not take up a sizable chunk of the first screen?

Headline

Does the headline stop readers dead in their tracks? (0–7)   _____

Does the headline read like an interesting editorial— instead of an ad? (0–7)   _____

Does the headline incorporate a compelling promise or point to a benefit that's important to the target audience? (0–2)   _____

Does the headline call out to the target audience? (0–1)   _____

Does the headline cause the reader to read the subheadline and/or the first paragraph of the web copy? (0–3) _____

Is this the best possible headline for the objective? (0–2) _____

Is this the best possible headline for the target audience? (0–2) _____

Is this the best possible headline for the product or service? (0–2) _____

Does the headline do *one or more* of the following: (0–1) _____

- ▶ Appeal to the emotions?
- ▶ Use *specifics?*
- ▶ Arouse curiosity?
- ▶ Make an announcement?
- ▶ Ask a question?
- ▶ Begin with the words *how to?*

First Paragraph or Opening Statement

Does the first paragraph cause the reader to read the second paragraph? (0–3) _____

Does the opening paragraph ask a compelling question that breaks preoccupation, grabs attention, and points to the result or benefit of the product or service? (0–2) _____

Style and Formatting

Is the web copy written in a conversational style? Does it use contractions, colloquialisms, and easy-to-read language instead of corporatespeak? (0–1) _____

Is it scannable? Does it do the following? (0–5)   _____

> ▶ Use bulleted lists to summarize content?

> ▶ Highlight (i.e., bold, italicize, underline) selected keywords to help scanners move through the web copy?

> ▶ Have meaningful subheads (versus amusing or clever ones)?

> ▶ Present one idea per paragraph?

> ▶ Use the inverted-pyramid style of writing (i.e., key points and conclusions presented first, followed by less important matters and background material)?

> ▶ Break paragraphs into two to four sentences?

> ▶ Incorporate interesting stories or case studies, significant facts, quotes, or statistics set off in boxes?

Body Copy

Is the body copy written in editorial (versus advertising) style? (0–3)   _____

Does the body copy lead readers down the intended sales path? (0–3)   _____

Was emotion injected into the body copy? Is the body copy built on proven emotional drivers such as anger, exclusivity, fear, greed, guilt, and curiosity? (0–3)   _____

Do all the parts of the body copy compel the reader to read from start to finish? Did you employ the questions "What's in it for me?" and "Who cares?" and "So what?"

after writing each sentence—and remove all sentences or phrases that don't satisfy those questions? (0–2) _____

Does the body copy employ the linear path—with minimal distractions and minimal clickable links that don't support the sales process? (0–5) _____

Does it use psychological devices that motivate prospects to buy? Have rational words been replaced with emotional words wherever possible? (0–3) _____

Does the body copy answer the question, "Will this product really work for me if I use it?" with an unequivocal "Yes!" Were all possible sales objections addressed? (0–2) _____

Is the writer of the website's information identified early in the body copy? Are reasons given for why the readers should believe the writer? (0–2) _____

Does the web copy convince readers that no other product or service can compare to the one that's being sold on the website? (0–2) _____

Offer, Testimonials, Bullets, Price, Guarantee, Bonuses, and Close

Is the offer crafted in an irresistible manner? Does it establish a unique selling proposition—and is that USP featured prominently on the web page? (0–3) _____

Does the web copy employ the use of testimonials? Are the testimonials strategically placed in areas where they reinforce the selling arguments? (0–3) _____

Does the web copy employ mouthwatering bullets? Do the bullets first state the benefit that readers will receive, followed up with either (1) a brief scenario of how their life will change when they get that benefit or (2) an injection of emotion, drama, or intrigue that elevates the desirability of that benefit? (0–3)   _____

Are free bonuses or gifts offered as an incentive to buy? (0–2)   _____

Does the close summarize the offer, employ a persuasive call to action, and inject a sense of urgency by giving compelling reasons to act now? Is the close written in a style that assumes the sale? (0–3)   _____

Does the web copy convince the reader that the product or service is worth the price? (0–2)   _____

Does the product or service being offered have a guarantee that removes the risk from the purchase? (0–3)   _____

Other Elements

Is there a mechanism to capture the web visitors' contact information? Does the opt-in offer feature an irresistible and easy way to compel the target audience to give up their contact information? (0–7)   _____

Does the web design layout and graphics support the web copy? (0–1)   _____

Does the order form include the following essential components? (0–3)   _____

- ▶ Check box
- ▶ Summary of offer, bonuses, and guarantee
- ▶ Price
- ▶ Assurance of secure ordering

▶ How the product or service will be delivered—and when

▶ Testimonial as reinforcement of purchase

TOTAL SCORE   _____

Note: To avoid having to manually add up your worksheet score, you can go to www.webCopywritingUniversity.com/formula.htm. That webpage enables you to simply plug in your scores, and the CGI script automatically calculates the total for you. (The CGI script is courtesy of Paul Galloway, www.PaulGalloway.com.)

Thomas Carruthers once said, "A teacher is one who makes himself progressively unnecessary." This formula is one of the devices I've used to make myself progressively unnecessary to my web copywriting students and clients. It allows you to dissect your own web copy (or your prospective clients' web copy), evaluate its selling ability, and make the necessary improvements—all in one fell swoop.

5

E-Mail Marketing:
The Internet's Killer Application

*It is not your customers' job to remember you. It is your
obligation and responsibility to make sure they don't have
the chance to forget you.*
—Patricia Fripp

Whenever I refer to *web copy*, I am using an umbrella term that includes not only website copy, but also e-mails that sell, opt-in offers, newsletters, e-zines, online ads (including pop-ups), autoresponder messages, free reports or promotional articles, search engine listings, signature files, and so on. These can represent as much as 90 percent of the sales you can make online.

Of all the components that make up the web copy mix, e-mail marketing is, in my opinion, the most important. For that reason,

I believe writing e-mail copy is crucial to your online success, whether you are a web copywriter or an Internet marketer.

TRAFFIC CONVERSION: TURNING VISITORS INTO CUSTOMERS

On the Internet, there are two fundamental ways of acquiring website sales: The first is to generate traffic to your website (*traffic generation*), and the second is to convert your website visitors into customers (*traffic conversion*).

Web copywriting is the primary element of traffic conversion. Make no mistake about it, as a web copywriter, your primary function is as a traffic converter. After all, what good is all the traffic in the world if you can't get visitors to your site do what you want them to do when they get there?

Traffic generators are those things that *drive* traffic to a website. Traffic generators include high search engine rankings, investing in pay-per-click search engines, affiliate marketing, e-zine advertising, joint-venture endorsements, and similar devices. There are thousands of ways to generate traffic. When you write marketing communications such as free reports, promotional articles, online ads, newsletters or e-zines, SIG files, and search engine listings, you assume the secondary role of traffic generator.

SIG File: Your Online Business Card

A signature file, also known as a SIG file, is, quite simply, your digital signature. It's the part of your e-mail message that appears at the very bottom that tells your story—who you are and what you do—or features whatever product or service you are promoting. A SIG file can be delivered in html or plain text.

Think of it as your online business card that you can use as a marketing tool, because it gives you the opportunity to advertise your website, your product, or your services with every e-mail you send at no cost to you.

Example:

John Smith
Director
ABC Hair Restoration Clinic
http://www.URL.com
Get your *free* report: "9 Facts You Must Know About Hair Loss—Before It's Too Late". Send a blank e-mail to 9facts@URL.com and the report will be sent to your e-mail box instantly.

Wagging the Website

Whenever I discuss e-mail marketing, I always mention *Wag the Dog,* a movie starring Robert de Niro as a political operative and Dustin Hoffman as a movie producer, whose characters come together to promote the sagging candidacy of the president. De Niro hatches a scheme that, with the help of Hoffman and the magic of Hollywood smoke and mirrors, fools the American public and the highest branches of the U.S. government into believing there is a war going on, setting in motion a huge chain of events. Thus, the tail (de Niro) is wagging the dog (the United States). The metaphor of the tail (a small, relatively insignificant appendage) wagging the dog, finds parallels in web commerce, particularly in the dynamic between e-mail and a website.

On the Internet, what do online businesses pay the most attention to and spend the most money on? The website, of course, because that's the highly visible component of the marketing mix. The website is where a business displays its products and services; it's where you close the sale and take the orders. E-mail, on the other hand, is not glamorous and is therefore viewed as merely a supporting component of the marketing process, which is a big mistake.

Most online entrepreneurs and writers overlook the significance of e-mail, and as a result, they write e-mails haphazardly, almost as an afterthought. They regard e-mail as something that supports the objectives of the website, or as a vehicle for customer service, or as a way to send out special announcements. In other words, they regard e-mail as a low-cost, inconsequential accessory to their web presence (like the tail of a dog, for instance).

While e-mail can and does make a fine supporting actor, used properly it can assume a starring role as the primary sales tool. E-mail can be used to direct what happens on your site, not vice versa. In essence, you can use e-mail to "wag the website."

Why Your E-Mail May Be More Important Than Your Website

I'm not suggesting by any means that a website is *not* important or that you should forget about putting one up. I am saying that if you rely exclusively on a website for your sales without using the power of e-mail to fuel those sales, your Internet business is not going to get very far.

E-mail marketing is a hot item in e-commerce. A layperson may think of commercial e-mail as spam, but to the marketing industry, e-mail is a gold mine that allows companies to speak personally and directly to prospects and customers and to carry on a relationship that contributes significantly to sales.

As you know, chances are, less than 1 percent of visitors to your site will ever buy your product or service. Even the best marketers with the most successful websites seldom convert more than 5 percent of their web visitors into customers when their website is their *only* marketing vehicle. That's why an opt-in mechanism is vital for capturing your visitors' contact information, developing a relationship with them, and, as a result, dramatically increasing the chance of ultimately making the sale.

In view of this, writing powerful e-mail copy is one of the most important skills required for doing business on the web. You should never write e-mail haphazardly. If you do, you'll be leaving a lot of money on the table. Here's why:

1. Virtually every person who is online sends and receives e-mail, but not everyone surfs the web. E-mail provides greater visibility for any Internet marketer. E-mail is also

a far better vehicle than a website for distributing and collecting information, as well as for developing a dedicated following.

2. Relationship marketing is at the very heart of all e-commerce. You simply can't build a relationship solely through your website, no matter how many interactive bells and whistles it has. E-mail, on the other hand, builds relationships. To produce an income, a website relies on people visiting and revisiting the site. You may have heard the saying, "The money is in the list." What it means is that when you leverage your relationship with the prospects in your database (your *list*), you are more likely to close a sale. That's because you give people a chance to know you and trust you. Even if your website gets only modest traffic, you can convert that traffic into more money than you can imagine through e-mail.

3. While it's true that a website makes the front-end sale, you'll be missing out on 90 percent or more of the potential profits if you don't use e-mail to fan the flames. The real selling starts after the first sale is made, by multiplying that one sale into many, many more sales through follow-up e-mails. This is why the *lifetime value* of the customer—not the first sale—is paramount.

Lifetime Value of a Customer. How do you calculate the lifetime value (LTV) of a customer? First, you figure out how many years your average customer does business with you (*customer lifetime*). Next, you estimate how much business you'll get from the average customer over that period of time (*sales per customer*). Then you factor in the number of referrals the average customer gives your company and multiply that by the percentage of those referrals that become customers. The formula will look like this:

Customer lifetime × sales per customer ×
number of referrals × percentage of referrals that
become customers = LTV

Let's plug in some hypothetical figures for an online bookstore:

Customer lifetime = 10 years
Sales per customer (per year) = $50
Number of referrals made by average customer = 4
Percentage of referrals that become customers = 26%

$$10 \times \$50 \times 4 \times 0.26 = \$520$$

Next, subtract the cost of books sold, say $403, and that gives the bookstore a gross margin (gross profit) of $117 per customer. That's the LTV of one customer to that bookstore.

If each customer has an LTV of $117, then the bookstore can easily determine how much it can reasonably spend to acquire each new customer and still make a profit over the lifetime of that customer. The profits probably won't come with the first sale. They may not even come in the first year, since the cost of acquiring a customer can be high, but if you build strong relationships and offer quality products and services, over the life of the customer, you should reap handsome rewards.

Note: If the bookstore sells other things, CDs, DVDs, stationery, greeting cards, and so on, each new category introduces new revenue streams and significantly increases the potential lifetime revenue from a customer.

4. E-mail helps you keep the customers you have. It costs much less to keep an existing customer than to acquire a new one. As mentioned in Chapter 3, according to *eMarketer,* it costs five to ten times as much to find a new customer as it does to retain an existing one. Additionally, loyal customers are more profitable to your business because they usually buy more of your company's products, are less sensitive to price, and often refer other customers. They usually take less of your customer service time because they're already familiar with your company.

5. An increasing number of traditional brick-and-mortar companies are discovering that a website is simply not sufficient for success in e-commerce. The Internet's killer application—e-mail—is now the primary vehicle for interactive marketing. Why? E-mail is a high-response-rate vehicle because it's in-your-face, immediate, and inexpensive. It sells, promotes, informs, creates buzz, acquires and retains customers, reinforces branding, and provides customer service all in one fell swoop.

Forrester Research reports that by the year 2005, the amount of commercial e-mail sent to U.S. consumers alone will grow to 40 times its 2002 volume. Therefore, it makes sense to maximize the impact of your e-mail messages, or you'll be buried alive in the mountains of e-mail that people get.

Having a mailing list of prospects does not mean you will automatically make money. That's *not* what "The money is in the list" means. The money is indeed in the list, but only if you know how to leverage that list through e-mail copy that deepens your relationship with the members of your list. You do this first and foremost by getting them to like you and gaining their trust.

In your e-mail, you can also use the same psychological devices you use when writing web copy, but if you fail to get your e-mail audience to like and trust you, you won't make sales. It's as simple as that.

How many times have you bought products that you didn't particularly like, want, or need just because you liked and trusted the people who were selling them to you. Ralph Wilson, who according to the *New York Times* is "among the best-known publishers and consultants who preach the responsible use of e-mail for marketing," exemplifies this premise. In addition to his reputation for providing outstanding marketing content in his website (Wilsonweb.com), he is well liked, trusted, and respected by hundreds of thousands of subscribers to his three e-mail newsletters (*Web Marketing Today, Doctor Ebiz, and Web Commerce Today*), something that undoubtedly contributes to the success of his online enterprises.

THE FRAME-OF-MIND MARKETING METHOD FOR WRITING E-MAILS
▼

Empathy is defined as the capacity to understand, be aware, be sensitive to, and vicariously experience the feelings, thoughts, and experiences of another person. Frame-of-mind marketing grows directly out of that feeling of empathy. While many seem to be born with that ability, the good news is that empathy is not a genetic trait, but rather, a skill that you can easily develop.

The ability to view things from the perspective of your audience is not only valuable in copywriting and marketing, but for all social interactions. The more sensitive you are to someone's frame of mind, the more persuasive you can be, the more rapport you can have with people, and, consequently, the more people will trust you and agree with you.

Let's examine the frame of mind of people who are in the process of opening their e-mail. The easiest way to do this is to put yourself in the shoes of your average e-mail recipient. Write down the thoughts that normally run through people's heads as they open their e-mail box. Here's an example of the typical thought process:

> *Okay, who sent me e-mail today?* They are curious and eager to receive e-mail. (A recent AOL/RoberASW study shows that people check their e-mail an average of 13.1 times a week.)

> *I'm busy and I just have enough time to read the good stuff.* They scan their in-box for (1) personal e-mail, (2) important business e-mail, and (3) other things that they have time to read, usually in that order.

> *Let me delete all the junk mail so that it doesn't clutter up my in-box.* People are inundated with commercial e-mail, free newsletters, and e-zines—and their forefinger is positioned over their mouse, ready to click on the Delete button. (Americans receive an average of more than 96

e-mails per week. Jupiter Communications reports that the number of commercial e-mails received by U.S. consumers will see a 40-fold increase by the year 2005.)

My e-mail box is my private, personal space, and I don't want strangers and salespeople invading my privacy. Their in-box is a sacred place, and they are protective of it, inviting only friends, relatives, colleagues, and selected business acquaintances to enter. Some people may have additional reasons, but these are nearly universal. Most of us probably feel the same way.

For this reason, the cardinal rule for writing successful e-mail copy is to review the frame of mind of your audience *before* writing a single word. Clearly, when we want to sell our ideas or products to others, we need to create rapport, and one good way to do this is by *aligning* ourselves with them, which simply means being like them. People develop a bond with you because they see a reflection of themselves in you. An effective way to do this is by *mirroring* the language in which your target audience communicates, which allows you to gain instant rapport with them. The result is that they instantly like and trust you, although they may not know why. Can you see how useful this can be in the selling process—online as well as offline?

People online are used to the up-close-and-personal language that is so prevalent in e-mail, instant messaging, and text messaging. There is a one-on-one, in-your-face kind of intimacy in e-mail, and you have to work with it and not against it. You must understand who your audience is and speak their language. At the same time, you should make it personal and conversational. Even if you are speaking to CEOs, you don't have to use the language of the boardroom. Speak to your reader's level of intelligence and comprehension, but keep it friendly.

Just as in writing copy for your website, don't begin your e-mail messages with formal corporatespeak: "We at Widgets. com have been in business for 15 years, and we are the industry's premier source of widgets." That kind of language doesn't only sound pompous, but it deliberately keeps your audience at arm's length. It's also boring, so your readers are likely to tune out. Furthermore, how does the fact that your company has existed for 15 years fill the needs of your audience? What's in it for them?

Breaking the Sales Barrier

There's another part of the equation that is rarely mentioned: Getting your prospects to like you is important, but what's even more important is letting your clients see that you like them. When that occurs, sales barriers really come down. When we know someone likes us, we believe that they won't cheat, lie to, or take advantage of us, but instead will give us the best possible arrangement or the best possible deal.

For this reason, it's crucial to write your e-mail as though you are writing to just one person that you're fond of, not 1,000, 10,000, or 100,000 at once. Don't speak *at* or *to* your reader, but *with* him or her.

Since your audience's e-mail box is a sacred place where only trusted people are welcome and invited, it is also the place where you can create the closest, strongest bond that can be forged between marketer and audience. You must never damage that bond by abusing your readers' trust in you. If they opted in to receive marketing tips from you, and if you don't deliver on that promise but instead give them sales pitches for various products, you blow it. If you treat their e-mail box as a dumping place for junk e-mail, you will also blow it.

People form opinions about you based on the e-mails you send them. Often, you don't know what those opinions are unless people happen to be vocal about them. Sometimes, people brag about the size of their mailing list, but as the saying goes, "It's not the number of eyeballs that matter, it's the frame of mind behind those eyeballs that really matters." Just because you have a list of 50,000 or 100,000 e-mail addresses doesn't mean that those people care a whit about you. I'd rather have a list of 1,000 devoted subscribers with whom I have a first-name relationship than 100,000 who couldn't care less about me. That's because I'd be more likely to make a significant number of sales from 1,000 loyal readers than from 100,000 strangers.

THE FUTURE OF E-MAIL MARKETING
▼

Anyone who has been online for any length of time is aware of the alarming proliferation of spam, or unsolicited commercial e-mail (UCE). The trend is expected to continue, as an increasing number of marketers, eager to cash in on the free marketing medium, exploit the situation without giving any thought to the bandwidth they are wasting and the people they are annoying. Add to that the growing fear of computer viruses, worms, scams, and pornography and you begin to understand the vigilance that organizations and the government are exercising to put a stop to spam.

On December 16, 2003, President George W. Bush signed into law the CAN-SPAM Act (Controlling the Assault of Non-Solicited Pornography and Marketing Act), which sets forth a framework of administrative tools and civil and criminal penalties to help America's consumers, businesses, and families fight spam. In addition, spam and virus filters have become standard on most e-mail servers, permanently blocking suspicious and obviously unsolicited e-mail.

Some people are predicting that, with the rise of flooded e-mail boxes and spam filters that block even legitimate opt-in messages, the demise of e-mail as a marketing and publishing channel is not far behind.

Is e-mail marketing on its way out? Not by a long shot. There's still a lot of marketing juice left in e-mail. At the end of August 2003, DoubleClick, a leading provider of tools for advertisers, direct marketers, and web publishers, released the findings of a study that found that e-mail campaigns conducted in the second quarter of 2003 had an increased open rate (to 38.8 percent), increased click-throughs (to 8.3 percent), and decreased bounces (to 11.5 percent). DoubleClick also reported that revenues generated by each e-mail and the purchase amounts remained steady compared to the previous year.

However, gone are the days when marketers could compose an e-mail message, push the Send button, and expect everyone on their mailing list to receive it. Marketers need to become more sophisticated about the medium in order to make their e-mail marketing as effective as it was prior to spam phobia. The rest of this chapter reveals some of the cybersmarts that you need to navigate the changing e-mail landscape.

HOW TO MAKE SURE YOUR E-MAIL IS DELIVERED

▼

Do you know the most important thing about e-mail? Many experienced marketers say, "Getting your e-mail opened." Actually getting your e-mail opened is the second-most-important thing. The most important is getting your e-mail delivered.

As a service to their users, more and more e-mail providers offer filters intended to radically reduce the amount of spam their users receive. What is a legitimate e-mailer to do? Let's say you send a mailing to your opt-in list, some of whom have services that block bulk mail and redirect it to the recipient's Bulk Mail box, the equivalent of sending it to Siberia. This happens frequently, especially if you have a huge mailing list. If your list is large, you may avoid such filters by breaking up your mailings into smaller chunks.

In addition to blocking bulk mail, a majority of e-mail programs allow their e-mail users to filter out spam and other junk mail. People can, for instance, ask to have e-mail that contains certain words such as *sex* or *girls* or *one-time mailing* in the subject or even in the body of the e-mail filtered from your in-box or sent to the trash bin. More and more people are availing themselves of such filtering capabilities. People can also filter out specific mailers. This is good and bad news, since they can also opt to let certain e-mailers in, but this often takes a specific action, and not all recipients are aware of this feature.

Some e-mail programs, like Outlook, automatically filter out e-mail that has the word *free* in all-capital letters in any part of the e-mail. If they find sales@anydomainname.com in the From field, they filter that out, too. Ditto for *extra income* or *for free* with a question mark or an exclamation point.

How to Avoid the Spam Blockers

Before you press the Send button on your promotional e-mail, newsletter, or e-zine—stop. Give it a once-over and see if it contains any of the following offending words and phrases:

Amazing	Money
Buy now	New
Congratulations	Opportunity
Dear friend	Order now
Free	Powerful
Great offer	Profit
Guarantee	Sale
Investment	Special Promotion
Maximize	Winner

In addition, customary phrases like "Click here" (or "Click below"), "Unsubscribe" or "To be removed" are also blocked, because these phrases are frequently used by spammers and other purveyors of unsolicited commercial e-mail.

If you've included any of these words—or any dollar signs, exclamation points, or anything in all capital letters, for that matter—in your outgoing e-mail, you may want to rethink what you have written.

That's because SpamAssassin (or similar systems) may inadvertently identify your e-mail as spam and block it from being delivered. SpamAssassin, one of the most popular open-source antispam applications, has several hundred spam filters and allows mail administrators to customize which e-mails get through and which ones are automatically blocked and sent to spam limbo, meaning they are redirected to the recipient's Bulk Mail bin or purged altogether.

Even if the e-mail you are sending is legitimate opt-in e-mail that the recipient has requested and wants to receive, it can be hijacked by e-mail providers or Internet service providers (ISPs), who are becoming increasingly vigilant about protecting their clients from junk e-mail.

You can see how easy it is to get caught in the crossfire and end up in the same dump as spammers. The sad fact is that some legitimate e-mail marketers and newsletter and e-zine publishers don't even realize that their e-mail is being rerouted to spam limbo, and they wonder why their click-through and conversion rates are dismal.

How do you get around this? You can either play by the rules and not use the offending words and phrases altogether, or you can devise creative ways to conceal the words and phrases from the spam radar. For example, you can insert symbols within the words; for example, use "fr^ee" or "fr*ee" instead of "free." Don't get too creative; your sentence or thought must still be understandable to your readers.

If you want your e-mail to be read and not filtered out as spam or junk mail, you must pay attention to these guidelines and keep up with the constant changes providers make.

Does Your E-Mail Test Positive as Spam?

My favorite strategy for sanitizing my e-mail of items that may trigger a false positive is by running it through Lyris's ContentChecker before sending it out. This is a free service that uses SpamAssassin's rules to rate your e-mail. You can find it at www.lyris.com/contentchecker.

When you get there, paste your text into the form provided on the website, and you'll instantly get a score. If your score is greater than five, it's an indication that your e-mail strongly resembles spam and might be blocked or filtered by major e-mail providers or ISPs. If it's less than five, you can be assured that your e-mail will be delivered without incident. Lyris will also send you a detailed analysis of what led to your score, identify the offending elements, and make recommendations on how to revise your message to conform to industry antispam criteria.

HOW TO WRITE E-MAIL THAT'S READ ▼

Let's assume your e-mail gets through those e-mail filters. How do you appeal to the actual e-mail recipients themselves? I've read tens of thousands of e-mails, and I've written thousands more over the past six years. I've found that the e-mails that do a great job of selling contain seven elements.

Seven Elements of E-Mails That Sell

Element 1: A Compelling Subject Line.   The subject line must be irresistible and must beg to be opened, *not* because of hype or overly commercial language, but because it is compelling. What's more, your subject line must not appear to be an advertisement, which, even if it somehow got through the filters, would have the same effect as asking readers to watch a TV commercial.

Remember that each of us is bombarded with an average of 3,500 commercial messages per day—from TV, billboards, radio, the Internet, and practically everywhere we turn. The last thing we want to see when we open our e-mail (or visit a website) is yet another ad. Yes, that applies even when we gave a company permission to send us e-mail.

Here's a simple exercise that will give you the best education you can get when it comes to writing subject lines that are impossible to ignore. This exercise puts you smack-dab in your prospects' shoes or, more precisely, in their frame of mind. Go to your e-mail box and check your incoming e-mail. You need to actually do this; don't be tempted to just do it mentally or you'll defeat the purpose of the exercise. This is positively eye-opening.

Once you have your e-mail in-box in front of you, what do you see? You see the sender, subject, date, and size columns. Where do your eyes go first? Some people glance at the sender column, but if you're like most people, you'll tend to scan the subject column to see which e-mail you want to open first, right? Which subject lines are you most likely to open first, and why? All the tests I've been involved in show that people are more likely to open those that have the appearance of personal e-mail versus commercial e-mail and those that have a friendly tone rather than a corporate, businesslike tone. Which of the following e-mails would you open first?

Subject: Online Marketing Gazette

Subject: Avon Spring Specials

Subject: Dinner's on me . . .

Subject: 30% Discount on Eyewear!

Subject: Holiday Bonanza

Subject: Save up to 70% off at Overstock, 40% at Amazon, and more!

I'm betting you'll open the e-mail with the subject line, "Dinner's on me . . ." first.

It's obvious which e-mails are personal and which are commercial, and it's easy to see that if the subject line of your e-mail looks like it's coming from a friend, it's more likely to be opened first.

Here are a few more examples of subject lines that give the appearance of personal e-mail; that is, they have a friendly tone rather than a corporate or commercial tone.

Subject: <fname>, this is barely legal . . .

Subject: This is unpublished . . .

Subject: Wait 'til you hear this . . .

Subject: Who said this?

Subject: This finally came . . .

Subject: Not sure if you got this?

Subject: This makes sense . . .

Subject: About your website, <fname> . . .

Subject: Here's what I promised . . .

Subject: Here's the formula . . .

Subject: I almost forgot . . .

Subject: Sorry, I goofed . . .

When your eyes zero in on the subject line, for instance, they also dart quickly (if not peripherally) to the sender field of the in-box. Therefore, the subject and the sender *must* agree with each other. Suppose you craft a subject line like the following in an attempt to trick the recipient into thinking it is a personal e-mail:

Subject: Hey, was that you I saw?

If the name in the sender field is "Internet Profits Weekly," your otherwise friendly and curiosity-provoking subject line is negated when your recipient realizes it's a ploy. Above all, be real.

Some say that this technique is deceptive because the recipient is not really your friend, but rather a prospect, a customer, a subscriber, or just someone who has opted into your list. The fact is, your e-mail recipient *should* perceive you as a friend. That's the heart of relationship marketing. That's the reason you ask viewers for their e-mail addresses in the first place—to start a relationship with them so they can get to know you, trust you, and eventually buy from you.

There's a very thin line between creating a riveting subject line and one that is deceptive. If you use trickery to get recipients to open your enticing message, they may bite once or twice, but when they recognize the pattern, the game's over. They're likely to ignore all future e-mails from you, and they may even ask to be removed from your list altogether. There are no hard-and-fast rules in e-mail. When you do your own intelligence work, the frame of mind of your audience will become apparent to you, and writing subject lines that are noticed will be a snap.

When you get a feel for the language used in e-mails that get maximum readership (personal e-mails), you've won half the battle. Reading this, you might think that creating a personal-sounding e-mail does not seem difficult. After all, you e-mail your friends all the time. Shouldn't it be a simple task to write marketing e-mails the same way? One would think so, but it's not. Somehow, when we sit down to write marketing e-mail, many of us try to be clever and creative, or we inject a big dose of marketese and, as a result, lose our friendly, personal tone, as we subconsciously switch to writing in a commercial or corporate style. That puts us way off the mark when it comes to e-mail communications.

To make matters interesting, I'm going to throw you a curve ball. I recently wrote a successful subject line that read, "Editorial Marketing: The New Profit-Building Model for E-Commerce Websites." That doesn't sound friendly or conversational at all. It's a straightforward "what's contained within," editorial-style subject line.

When sent to the appropriate target audience, it works because it suggests a benefit to the reader and arouses curiosity (new profit-building model). Furthermore, it reads like an editorial, not an ad (even though the body of the e-mail promotes a telecourse, i.e., a course delivered via telephone bridge lines). This subject line appeals to the audience's information-seeking mind-set. Again, there are no hard-and-fast rules—only guidelines. What is true is that it's essential to pay attention to the frame of mind of your audience and the medium in which they will be viewing your message, and to assess the impact you're making. Here are a couple of examples of editorial-style subject lines designed for specific target audiences:

Subject: Venture Capitalists Explain How to Get Funded

Subject: Inside: Exclusive Interview with Shania Twain

Personalizing E-Mails—Not All It's Cracked Up to Be. We've established that, above all, e-mail subject lines need to be as friendly, human, and personable as possible, but do they need to be personalized? I have long advocated personalizing subject lines, but I was in for a shock recently when I opened my e-mail box and found five e-mails from five different senders with the following subject lines:

Subject: Maria, this Friday

Subject: Maria, will you be part of this test?

Subject: Maria, you're in . . .

Subject: Maria, your account

Subject: Maria, last chance!

The e-mails came from five different senders. That was a real eye-opener. I realized that the tactic of using the recipient's first name as a way of personalizing the subject line had become so widespread that instead of making me want to open the e-mails, it made them candidates for deletion! Any one of these subject lines on its own might have been an effective device for getting people to open your e-mail, but when viewed in the context of the recipient's in-box, it lost its punch.

This may seem minor, but it has major repercussions for your marketing, not only in terms of this particular device, but as it applies to other techniques that might, over time, become overused.

What would happen if you weren't constantly in tune with your audience's frame of mind, or weren't paying attention to the trends as they emerge? If you rely on what others are doing and continue to blindly use the same tactic, your e-mails will fail miserably, and you might never know why your response rates dropped.

Part of deciphering the frame of mind of your prospects is observing what they're wising up to, what they're becoming immune to, and which tactics are no longer working. You will be well served if you observe what e-mail spammers are doing. Spammers often resort to devices that attempt to disguise the fact that their e-mails are unsolicited (using phrases like "at your request"). Those devices start becoming recognizable to your target readers, who then begin ignoring or deleting the messages. If those devices start to resemble yours, you need to adjust lest your e-mails be mistaken for spam.

Crafting the All-Important Subject Line. You recall that I mentioned the most important element of a website: the *first screen.* In an e-mail, the subject line is the most important element.

Direct Magazine reported that an American leatherware firm sent out a marketing e-mail to its mailing list and accidentally omitted the body copy. Right. Their e-mail was sent to their entire list with nothing but the subject line. Much to their surprise, that mailing generated the largest response rate they had ever had! When writing subject lines, keep these things in mind:

▶ *This.* The word *this* in the subject line of an e-mail is proven to get e-mail recipients to open their e-mail.

   This is barely legal . . .

   This is so powerful because it arouses the recipients' curiosity, and they must open the e-mail to find out what *this* is. Of course, not all subject lines containing the word *this* will be opened. For example, "This is the best moneymaker in the world . . ." would most likely be recognized as spam and immediately deleted. Other powerful e-mail openers are *here* and *about your* . . .

▶ *Ellipsis points.* Whenever possible, I use ellipsis points (three dots) at the end of my subject lines. This creates a sense of incompleteness (you're planting a dissonance element or Zeigarnik effect), which makes readers rush to open your e-mail.

▶ *Incomplete thoughts.* Presenting an incomplete thought in the subject line, especially about a topic of particular interest to your target audience, causes what I call a "brain itch." Scientifically, it arouses the *reticular activating system* (RAS) in the brain, which is the part of the brain that dislikes incomplete information and does not rest until it finds the information it needs to close a topic. This "brain itch" can be relieved only when the reader opens the e-mail to complete the thought. The thought, of course, must relate to the topic of your e-mail. Otherwise, recipients will click open your e-mail just to satisfy their curiosity, then click away when they realize it was simply a ploy to get their attention.

Words to Avoid Putting in the Subject Line.   Strangely enough, some of the attention-grabbing words that you would use on a website are some of the very words you must avoid in an e-mail subject line:

Buy	Power
Discount	Powerful investment
Free, Maximize	Profit
Money opportunity	Sale
New	Special

Words like these reek of advertising or commerce, when your goal is to appear friendly and personal. While these are the magic words advertisers and direct marketers swear by and use liberally in their copy, they are not effective when used in e-mail. This is an area in which what works well in offline marketing (direct mail, radio and TV, print ads or infomercials) does not work well on the web. In fact, chances are, these words will fail miserably on the web, not to mention censored by spam filters.

Permission-Based E-mail: Not a License to Be Bland.   I'm often asked whether it is advisable to put the name of the company or newsletter in the subject line of an e-mail. My answer is that permission-based e-mail doesn't give you the liberty to be bland.

Much has been said about the recipient's "permission" being the foundation of e-mail marketing. Apparently, 92 percent of U.S. consumers feel positively toward companies that ask their permission before sending them information (according to a nationwide survey by Brann Worldwide, a marketing agency). Based on this, some marketers believe that the subject line of their e-mail must identify who they are in order to remind the recipient that the e-mail contains requested information.

In an environment where most e-mail recipients usually can't remember whether or not they asked for this or that information, you don't have the luxury of playing it safe by using a bland subject line that consists of nothing but the name of your company or newsletter. The objective of the subject line is to give the recipient a compelling reason to open your e-mail *now*. Instead of using the all-important subject line to state *who* you are, it's far better to use the sender field or the first sentence to identify yourself.

Element 2: The First Sentence.   The next thing you need is an opening line that identifies who you are and establishes rapport. Your e-mail must have a real person behind it; it can't be a faceless piece of communication. You can start by saying something that you would say to a friend. I've seen an Australian newsletter publisher, for example, start an e-mail by describing the wonderful weather they are having in Australia and briefly describing the idyllic setting where he lives and works. A famous Internet marketer started an e-mail by saying that he just got back from a successful trip, followed by a short description of that trip. Brevity is the key; just a couple of ice-breaking sentences should suffice.

Some copywriters and marketers skip this seemingly insignificant gesture because they want to get to the point and not waste their audience's time. As a result, they miss the opportunity to bond with their readers and gain rapport with them. Some of the most successful e-mails are the ones that elicit the reaction from people that makes them say, "I feel like I know you!" This is your opportunity to get your audience to like you, and if they like you they're more inclined to buy from you.

Element 3: Stay on Point.   This is the gist of your marketing message or the promise of a benefit to come. A good way to do this is by using a journalists' device called the *inverted pyramid* (an upside-down triangle with the narrow tip pointing down and the broad base at the top). The broad base represents the most significant, newsworthy information, and the narrow tip the least important information. Following this method, you put the most important information at the beginning and the least important information at the end of your e-mail. As with most journalism, brevity and clarity get high marks, so get right to the point. Your readers are busy, and they don't want you wasting their time.

Whatever you do, don't make the mistake many Internet entrepreneurs make and start your e-mail with a lengthy reminder that the e-mail is not unsolicited, that the recipient has agreed to receive your mailing or newsletter, and then offer instructions on how to opt out. While this statement acknowledges the permission-based aspect of your relationship, it wastes the first screen of your e-mail, which is the prime area for starting your sales process. Put instructions for opting out at the end of your message.

Element 4: Just One Message. Don't litter your e-mail with a slew of subjects and topics. Stick to a single message so that you can lead your reader down your intended sales path.

When average recipients receive an e-mail, particularly a lengthy one, they don't read it sequentially. They scan it looking for things that may interest them. If three or four topics grab their attention, they make a mental note of them and start reading the one that interests them most. As they read that part of your e-mail, the Zeigarnik effect kicks in, and their brain is unable to pay full attention to what they're reading. Various other ideas start competing for attention. This can easily work against you, especially if you are trying to sell something. Not only will you *not* have your readers' full attention, but also they are not likely to go down your intended sales path or take action of any kind, because the brain is compelling them to read the other things that attracted them.

Multiple messages in a single e-mail, combined with the fact that e-mail readers have short attention spans, makes for an unholy alliance when it comes to e-mail marketing.

Element 5: Provide Value. Give your e-mail recipients something of value in return for their undivided attention. This could be something free or at a discount, or some useful information or a special offer.

Element 6: The Benefit. It's not enough just to tell your readers what your offer is; you must demonstrate how it will benefit them. An easy way to do this is to state the offer and follow it up with ". . . so that you can [fill in the blank]." A travel website, for instance, can say, "Try our free fare-tracking service so that you can be informed weekly of all the unpublished, hard-to-find bargain fares to Boston—without having to scour the web."

Element 7: A Call to Action. Many e-mail marketers go to great lengths to create well-crafted e-mails that make a compelling selling argument about their product or service, but at the last moment, when the prospect is just about ready to take the next step, they drop the ball by failing to ask the prospect to take action. The action can be a request to click, sign up, register, or buy, but whatever it is, you must make sure you tell the reader what to do next. This is true not only for your e-mails but for your website and *all* marketing communications.

PUT THE COMPETITIVE EDGE INTO YOUR E-MAIL MARKETING

Forrester Research analyst Jim Nail underscored how important it is for e-commerce players to use e-mail to create a dialogue and deepen intimacy with customers in order to maintain the response rates that e-mail marketing often enjoys. He emphasized the importance of starting slowly and gradually building rapport, which allows you to gain additional personal information that in turn helps you fine-tune your marketing and sales message.

Creating a dialogue, deepening intimacy, and building rapport takes us back to frame-of-mind marketing and the importance of knowing your prospects' and customers' frame of mind. Once you've identified and written down all the aspects of your own list members' frame of mind, you are ready to write an effective e-mail.

The following technique takes the struggle out of writing e-mail.

Step 1: Write down the three words that best describe the message you're trying to convey. Not a three-word sentence, mind you, but three individual words or phrases that summarize the thought you are trying to communicate—for example, a smell, a benefit, an emotion, a color, a mood, a texture, a sound, a flavor, an adjective that describes your message. If I were writing a letter about a hair restoration product, I might choose *patent, scientific,* and *side effects.* Or maybe *clinical, success rate,* and *track record.*

Your three words help narrow your focus and keep you grounded. After you select the words, start writing your e-mail letter, paying attention to these simple rules:

▶ Focus on the frame of mind of your audience, and write in a way that appeals to that frame of mind.

▶ Write the way you speak.

▶ Don't try to be creative or formal.

▶ Write the letter as though you're writing it to one person only—and that person is your friend.

Step 2: Give yourself five minutes to write the letter, making sure you use your three key words in the letter. *Don't* edit the letter as you write. Here's a trick that will make editing your letter painless: When you are finished writing, e-mail it to yourself. The perspective you'll gain from this experience is priceless. You'll see firsthand how you'd perceive your subject line relative to other subject lines in your in-box. Would *you* pick it out among the rest of your incoming e-mail? Would you open it and read the letter? You'll read it in a whole new light: from the point of view of your recipient. With every sentence, ask yourself, "Is this something that I would say to a friend?" If the answer is no, revise what you've written.

Similarly, you will discover the nuances of language and whether you've succeeded in gaining rapport and persuading your prospects into taking the action you want them to take. All the rough areas that need work will become apparent, and you will see exactly what needs to be fixed.

Adapt as Your Audience's Frame of Mind Changes

When you send a series of e-mails to your list, the recipients' frame of mind is slightly altered with each mailing, as your previous communications influence their expectations and predispositions. They may have warmed up to you and begun to trust you more, or, if you have misread their frame of mind, maybe just the opposite.

All too often, marketers assume that each e-mail gets the same kind of attention as those that went before. This is a mistake. You must never write in a vacuum or regard each e-mail as an isolated piece. You must think of each e-mail as part of a conversation in an ongoing relationship.

When you have a good grasp of your prospects' frame of mind at every stage, you are in a better position to monopolize their attention. Since you know what your prospects' predispositions and expectations are, you have the opportunity to find ways to engage them. For instance, you can use the element of surprise to delight or intrigue them, or you can find ways to arouse their curiosity in order to make them look forward to future e-mails.

The variations are practically infinite. Just consider the unique frame of mind of your own list members and you can come up with ideas that may have never occurred to you before and that are custom-made for your list.

Using E-Mail to Get Attention

Earlier we discussed the reticular activating system (RAS) in relation to subject lines of e-mails and the brain's need for closure, its need to complete incomplete thoughts. The RAS, in essence, is the attention center in the brain. It is the key to turning on the brain and is considered the center of motivation. It determines what we pay attention to.

Here's an example of how the reticular activating system (RAS) works: Do you remember the last time you decided to buy a new car? Let's say you decided that you wanted to buy a Ford Explorer. All of a sudden you started seeing more Ford Explorers than you'd ever seen before. That's not because people are buying Explorers in record numbers; it's because the RAS of your brain made you aware of them, whereas you previously ignored them.

The RAS receives thousands of stimuli and messages every second, and since it is not possible for our brains to pay attention to everything, the RAS filters or blocks out most of the messages, allowing only certain ones to come to our attention. You can immediately see how valuable it would be if you could get your e-mail messages to rise above the avalanche of messages that your recipients receive. Here are some of the ways you can stimulate your prospects' RAS in order to transition them to a receptive frame of mind:

1. *Ask your reader to write something down.* The act of writing something down helps trigger the RAS. In her book, *Write It Down, Make It Happen,* Henriette Anne Klauser wrote, "Writing triggers the RAS, which in turn sends a signal to the cerebral cortex: 'Wake up! Pay attention! Don't miss this detail!' " What you ask readers to write down will depend on the nature of the product or service that you sell. I have a client who is a director of a discount buying club that offers up to 18 percent in rebates whenever members purchase from among 200-plus online stores with more than 250,000 products. An e-mail I wrote to encourage members to shop in these stores included these words, "I'm sure you're eager to get started, so make a list of all the things you need to buy in the next three months, such as [I listed a dozen

items]," and concluded with the words, "Go ahead and write them all down."

The simple act of writing down the items puts them at the forefront of your readers' minds and makes them receptive to go the next step and do what you ask them to do. Think back on your own experience. Isn't it true that whenever you had a written list of things you needed to buy (whether you carried that list with you or not), your mind subconsciously zeroed in on those items when they came into your field of vision? Your mind may have tuned out those things had you not written them down.

2. *Create a small, but entertaining or interesting, activity.* This provides a refreshing diversion from the usual barrage of commercial e-mail. Make sure the activity leads up to a well-crafted marketing message that invites readers to click through to your website or otherwise carries them along your intended sales path. When you lead off with a noncommercial activity, you get recipients to agree to something. When you subsequently get them to click through to your website, that's another *yes*. In effect, you are breaking a large buying decision into several manageable steps to which the reader can say "Yes!" Professional salespeople use this technique all the time.

One marketer who sells software for installing website audio sends out an e-mail inviting the recipient to send a free personalized audio postcard to three friends. It is an ingenious (and fun) activity that also demonstrates the ease of producing an audio recording, displays its excellent sound quality, and thereby paves the way to the sale of the software.

3. *Invite your recipient to participate in a quick poll or a one-question survey.* This is an involvement device that gets your readers to pay attention to a subject on which you want them to focus. The subject of the poll or survey should be one that is of particular interest to your list members, as well as one that gives you the opportunity to segue into your marketing message. As an incentive, you may offer to give participants access to the poll or survey results.

4. *"Please forward."* The Association for Interactive Marketing (AIM) discovered a technique for encouraging pass-along readership of its newsletter. AIM simply added "Pls. Forward" to the end of its newsletter subject lines. The association reports that this little device has more than doubled its circulation numbers.

What *Really* Works on the Internet Sometimes Doesn't

There are rarely absolute truths when it comes to Internet marketing. There are only conditional truths, based on the frame of mind of the marketplace or your audience. What was true yesterday, last week, or last year may not be true today.

With direct mail, when you track and test your mail pieces and identify your control piece, you can roll out the control piece and virtually predict how much money you will make with mathematical certainty. On the Internet, results are not as predictable, because things change rapidly. While I'm an advocate of tracking and testing online, my test results may or may not apply to you, and you should be wary of those who offer sweeping generalizations.

No one website strategy, e-mail tactic, or marketing message works all the time. Ultimately, you alone can determine what will and will not work, depending on the frame of mind of your own audience and the results of your own tracking and testing. There are e-mail marketing services that have the ability to evaluate the effectiveness of your e-mail campaigns by tracking how many of your e-mails were opened, replies, length of time opened, specific links clicked on, bounces, unsubscribes, and even orders completed. In my opinion, these services are invaluable not only because they show unequivocally what's working and what's not working, but because they also enrich your knowledge of your audience's frame of mind in real time.

6

Online Marketing Communications:

It's What You Do After People Visit Your Website That Counts

If you advance confidently in the direction of your dreams,
and endeavor to live the life which you have imagined, you
will meet with a success unexpected in common hours.
—Henry David Thoreau

Online marketing communications play a low-profile but none-theless pivotal role in the Internet marketing arena. Principal among these is the opt-in offer, the crafting of which is often more important than website copy for reasons that will become clear as you progress through this chapter. Irresistible autoresponder e-mails are yet another essential aspect of online marketing com-munications, because effective follow-up frequently spells the dif-ference between mediocre and outstanding sales. Finally, learning how to write free reports, promotional articles, newsletters, e-zines, online ads, signature files, and banner copy complete the basic components that comprise the web marketing mix. In this chapter, we look at each of these marketing communications and how to create killer copy for each.

THE OPT-IN OFFER: YOUR MOST IMPORTANT ASSET
▼

Converting web visitors into customers is rarely completed during the website visit, but by crafting an irresistible opt-in offer and following up with e-mail messages designed to build rapport and a relationship with the prospects, conversion rates of 15 to 25 percent (and sometimes greater) can be achieved.

My friend and fellow copywriter, Alex Mandossian, created a website (www.marketingwithpostcards.com) that attracts only about 100 unique visitors per day, but as many as 23 percent of his web visitors take him up on his opt-in offer to download three free chapters of his course. Because he has constructed his follow-up autoresponder e-mails effectively, he averages about $27,298 per month in revenues from his website. That results from just 100 unique visitors per day.

Capturing contact information is fundamental to the success of any business enterprise. As web marketer, entrepreneur, or copywriter, your primary goal, at the very least, should be capturing your web visitors' e-mail addresses. Without this information, you have in effect wasted all the time, money, and effort it took to get them to your website. For this reason, I can't overemphasize that constructing your opt-in offer is infinitely more important than crafting the offer for your primary product.

It's apparent, therefore, that you need to make your opt-in-offer copy as compelling as possible in order to convince visitors to give you this personal information. A good way to do this is by providing a benefit that gives visitors an incentive to give you their e-mail address. One method is to ask them to sign up for a free report (with an irresistible title), a free newsletter, a free course, free product, free chapters of your book—in other words, something that requires no financial commitment.

The following opt-in offer was designed as an exit pop-up (a window that pops up when the visitor leaves the site). The objective of this opt-in offer is to capture the contact information of as many web visitors as possible so that, through a series of follow-up autoresponder e-mails, prospects can be encouraged to sign up for a DHS Club discount buying membership. (See Figure 6.1.)

"How to Pay Less for Almost Everything" is a title that appeals to the target audience of the DHS Club website, which consists of people who like to save money on everything they purchase. The opt-in offer is designed to prequalify prospects. In this case, it means that anyone who signs up to receive this free report is interested in getting discounts and saving money on purchases and therefore is someone who might also be interested in signing up for a paid membership to the discount buying club to get even more discounts on a wider variety of products and services.

"How to Pay Less for Almost Everything"
The world's best *bargain hunters* and haggle hounds reveal their **secrets** for easily finding the *lowest prices* on things you buy everyday. Once you learn these simple, but **ingenious** strategies for getting more and spending less, it's like having given yourself a **20% (or more) pay raise** -- tax-free!

Send for this **FREE report** today. Simply fill in your name and address in the form below -- and this **valuable** report will be sent to your e-mail box automatically *within minutes*!

[Your contact information will be handled with the *strictest confidence*, and will never be sold or shared with third parties.]

☐	Send me my FREE report now.
Email address:	
First Name:	
Last Name:	

Add Address

Figure 6.1

Five Keys to an Opt-in Offer That's Impossible to Refuse

In addition to creating an offer that prequalifies prospects, there are five elements that winning opt-in offers contain:

1. Compelling title that speaks to the needs of your target audience

2. Appetizing benefits

3. Ease and speed (instant gratification)

4. Assurance of privacy

5. Form for obtaining e-mail address and, at least, a first name

Notice that the opt-in offer for the DHS Club satisfies all of these:

1. It has a compelling title ("How to Pay Less for Almost Everything") that speaks to the needs of the target audience (people who like saving money on all their purchases).

2. It offers appetizing benefits the recipients will receive (secrets for easily finding the lowest prices on things they buy every day).

3. It offers ease and speed. (The valuable report will be sent to their e-mail box automatically *within minutes.*)

4. It offers an assurance of privacy. (Their contact information will be handled with the strictest confidence and will never be sold or shared with third parties.)

5. It includes a form that captures the e-mail address and the first name.

A free subscription to a newsletter or e-zine is the most common item featured in online opt-in offers. There was a time when free subscriptions were desirable, but because practically everyone is offering a free newsletter or e-zine nowadays, people are not as eager as they once were to sign up for them. A growing number of people regard free newsletters and e-zines as contributors to their already cluttered e-mail boxes, particularly since the content of most leaves a lot to be desired.

Since the objective of an opt-in offer is to get as many web visitors as possible to sign up, you must offer something irresistible that people can't wait to get their hands on right away, something that offers instant gratification instead of a promise of monthly (or weekly) issues of publications of dubious value. Examples of these are a must-have free report, a free software download, or a free e-book, to name a few. Here are examples of Mark Joyner's most successful opt-in offers:

> Free report: "How I Made $4 Million on a $0 Ad Budget" (a four-page 1,267-word article)
>
> Free software download: Ezine Assistant—software that formats outgoing e-mail copy to ensure that it looks professional (i.e., without line breaks in all the wrong places) for every type of e-mail program
>
> Free e-book: *Search Engine Tactics* (this has been downloaded more than a million times and captured as many e-mail addresses)

You conceivably could offer a free newsletter that gives irresistible content, but I don't recommend it as the *primary* opt-in offer. I don't mean to imply that newsletters and e-zines are no longer viable marketing vehicles. On the contrary, when written effectively, they're still a major marketing communication by which companies stay connected to their prospects and customers. However, for the purpose of capturing the contact information of as many web visitors as possible, they should be regarded as *secondary* opt-in vehicles.

Presenting the Offer

An opt-in offer doesn't have to be in the form of a pop-up window. It can appear as part of a webpage. An abbreviated form of it can even be featured in an online ad, embedded in an e-mail signature file, or announced in discussion boards and forums. Here is an example of an online ad designed for tax preparers that incorporates an opt-in offer:

> Discover *The Best Tax Break* that can give your small business and Schedule C clients a net tax savings of $1,800 to $2,125 every year. Send for the Free Report that reveals this secret by sending a blank e-mail to report@domain.com.

HOW TO WRITE IRRESISTIBLE AUTORESPONDER E-MAILS ▼

Once you have captured the names of those people you enticed with the free report, what do you send them via e-mail? Send a series of follow-up e-mails using the autoresponder mechanism.

Quick Primer on Autoresponders

Most web hosts allow you to use e-mail addresses that automatically call up a prewritten e-mail that you upload to their server. When someone sends an e-mail to that address, your web host's server automatically sends out the prewritten e-mail that you uploaded. For example, if you send a blank e-mail to tamsbs@sitesell.net, you will automatically receive a five-day e-mail course titled "Affiliate Masters Course" (by Ken Evoy, author of *Make Your Site Sell*) on how to become a high-earning affiliate. That in a nutshell is the concept of an autoresponder.

Taking this a step further, there are e-mail programs, shopping cart programs, and services that allow you to send a series of prewritten e-mails to your opt-in list at predetermined intervals, say, every three days. This automates the follow-up system for you.

Marketers often use the rule of seven, which has its roots in radio and television advertising. The rule states that prospects must see or hear your message seven times before they consider buying. It's not a hard-and-fast rule, just a rule of thumb. It applies not only to radio and television advertising, but to online advertising as well. When you use autoresponders to send out seven or more marketing e-mails at predetermined intervals, you increase the chances of the prospect buying from you.

Crafting Autoresponses to Your Opt-In Offer

Step 1: Get recipients to *consume* what you just gave them for free. What's the use of getting them to download three free chapters, receive a free report, or download free software if you don't get them to read or use it? Most people don't read or use what they send for. If you don't get them to read the free chapters, they'll never buy the entire course. If you don't get them to read the free report that shows them how to save money, you'll never get them to sign up to join the discount buying club.

In the first autoresponse I developed to send to those who signed up to receive "How to Pay Less for Almost Everything," I wrote:

> Somewhere in the free report you received is the "best-kept secret" for amazing savings that is truly simple and effortless.
>
> Most people miss it altogether because they skim through the report too fast—and yet it's probably the most important thing you can do in *1 minute flat* that can give you cash back on all your purchases at hundreds of major stores. Well, I won't keep you in suspense any longer. I'll point out exactly where that best-kept secret is hidden. It's in the 11th paragraph of the report.

Later in the e-mail, I wrote:

> To save you the trouble of having to find your free report, I've made it easy for you and given you the link below. Click on the link and check it out to see how simple it is for you to get similar savings on your purchases.
> http://www.domain.com

Step 2: With every subsequent e-mail, highlight a different benefit of your product(s) or service(s) and explore a different angle that slides smoothly into a compelling reason why the recipient needs to buy what you're selling.

The succeeding autoresponses in the "How to Pay Less for Almost Everything" series extolled different virtues of the shopper's club. Autoresponse number 2 reminded prospects that they could receive 30 to 70 percent discounts on the things they bought that week or month and, in addition, would receive free shipping. The third reminded them that they would receive rebates on all the purchases made by friends and family that they bring into the club. The fourth stressed that they were losing money each day they were not a member. Autoresponse number 5 told the engaging story of how the shopper's club started out in a small apartment above a garage, how its membership grew to more than 3 million, and how the combined buying power of its members means more savings to the prospect.

Crafting Autoresponses to Customers

Autoresponder e-mails are not only for prospects. You can create a series specifically for purchasers of your product or service to help multiply one sale into a stream of ongoing back-end sales at the same time it reinforces the sale and minimizes buyer's remorse (and returns).

The autoresponse series that I wrote to purchasers of a $995 program for starting a promotional products distributorship consisted of seven e-mails. The first reinforces the sale by featuring the success story of the owner of a printing business who bought the program, relating how he used what he learned in the program to earn a six-figure income after only seven months and how he eventually closed down his printing business to concentrate on promotional products full-time. The e-mail also suggests a quick, three-step action plan for the customer to follow to get his or her promotional business or profit center up and running quickly.

The second e-mail starts with yet another success story. This time of a woman who used the program to obtain her first order, amounting to $13,000. To learn her strategy, the reader is told to listen to the first tape of the two-tape course that came with the program. The remaining three autoresponse e-mails continue in a similar vein, each offering another success strategy and reinforcing the advantages of the program.

How to Format Your E-Mails for Optimum Readability

The readability of your e-mails is of utmost importance if your e-mails are to achieve their purpose of leading the prospect down the intended sales path. There's nothing worse than sending an e-mail with jagged, uneven lines (a long line, followed by a short line, then another long line followed by another short line, and so on). This occurs when your e-mail is in one format and your recipient's is in another.

To avoid this, you should format your outgoing e-mail so that it is readable by all e-mail programs. Set your line lengths to 60 characters (including spaces) per line so that the lines don't automatically wrap. Don't panic. You don't have to waste time counting characters and manually adding hard returns when a line reaches 60 characters. Instead, you can use a program called Ezine Assistant (download it free from www.ezineassistant.com).

HOW TO WRITE FREE REPORTS AND PROMOTIONAL ARTICLES

▼

Writing free reports or promotional articles can be one of the most profitable things you can do to promote the product or service you're selling on your website. When you write a free report or promotional article, you can use it not only as your opt-in offer, but you can also offer its content to websites, newsletters, and e-zines. The more it is picked up, the more traffic it will pump to your website.

Information is the Internet's main commodity, so when you have good content to offer, you'll find many takers. A promotional article titled "Warning: Do Not Buy a Computer Until You Read This—Or You Might Get Ripped Off" offered compelling reasons for consumers to be wary when buying a computer. It listed six of the sneakiest—and even illegal—schemes employed by unscrupulous computer vendors to take advantage of unsuspecting buyers. Nowhere in the article was there a commercial slant; it consisted of only solid, informative content. The author's byline, however, provided the opportunity to plug her book about how to save $500 or more on a computer purchase.

To achieve its goals, a free report or promotional article must:

▶ Provide useful, bona fide content related to the product or service you're offering.

▶ Be written in a way that positions you as an expert in your field.

▶ Include a byline or resource box that points to your website.

The important thing to remember is that the body of the report or article must contain information of value to your target audience. The sales pitch is introduced only after identifying the author (you) in the byline or resource box. Most e-zine and newsletter publishers are looking for articles of between 500 and 800 words. Some publishers are very strict about your article not being a sales pitch in disguise.

I've seen an article titled "Nobel Prize Winner Discovers the Cause of Cancer—and How to Cure It" employed as a promotional piece by a coral calcium vendor. It starts by stating that Dr. Otto Warburg won two Nobel Prizes for discovering the cause of cancer and goes on to explain his theory. Only at the end does the vendor conclude that its product contains the necessary factors to prevent cancer. The one-page, 252-word article is an example of a promotional piece that provides information of value to its target audience without appearing commercially slanted. It's the kind of article that would be accepted for publication by e-zine and newsletter publishers looking for content relating to health, antiaging, or longevity.

The key to writing successful free reports or promotional articles is to keep them factual, unbiased, informative, and, most important, engaging. Make them revelatory, if that's possible with your subject matter. Avoid making a sales pitch, no matter how skillfully you think you can disguise it, and, above all, never identify the name of your product or service in the article. That's a telltale sign of self-promotion. Finally, don't use superlative adjectives and phrases (*amazing, incredible, world's best, taking the world by storm, spreading like wildfire, causing quite a stir,* etc.), which will expose your commercial intent.

GUIDELINES FOR WRITING NEWSLETTERS AND E-ZINES

▼

For the following reasons, publishing your own newsletter or e-zine is one of the best and most economical ways to build traffic (and sales):

1. *It's free.* Anyway, it's almost free. It costs little or no money to produce and deliver a newsletter or e-zine no matter how many people you send it to.

2. *It's profitable.* You can easily build rapport and credibility with your subscribers and quickly be acknowledged as an expert in your field through your newsletter or e-zine. In turn, anything you promote or endorse will have a greater impact than any advertisement.

3. *You have a captive audience.* One thing that people consistently do online is check their e-mail. I recently read a statistic that people check their e-mail 13.2 times per week, an activity that's second only to the number of times people brush their teeth in a week. People may not have time to visit the millions of websites that are out there, but most people do check their e-mail regularly and read selected items in their e-mail box. Your e-zine would therefore be more likely to have the undivided attention of your audience than would your website.

4. *It keeps you in touch.* Your newsletter or e-zine enables you to stay in constant contact with your audience, and it constantly puts your business in front of your prospects. It is a great way to remind people to do business with you or to visit your website, without sounding like an ad.

Since newsletters and e-zines are all over the web, you need to make sure you offer one that has unique content of great interest to your target audience. More important, to attract the most subscribers, your offer must have a compelling promise, but at the same time be able to deliver on that promise.

The newsletter offer of Affirm Ware reads: "Join the millions of people around the world who have discovered the power of affirmations. Send for your FREE SUBSCRIPTION to 'Affirmations of the Mind' Tips and Techniques Self-Help Newsletter, the premier publication for self-improvement and personal growth. Each issue contains *powerful sample affirmations* that have been tested and proven to get results."

As with all e-mail writing, don't be tempted to put the whole kitchen sink in your newsletter or e-zine. While providing value is something to strive for, don't be tempted to litter your publication with a multitude of subjects and topics. It may not always be easy to stick to a single message in a multipart publication, so the best thing to do is to have a *cohesive theme* that will enable you to lead your readers down your intended sales path.

Needless to say, the content you offer in your newsletter or e-zine must be related to the products or services that you are selling. Make sure you always provide bona fide content. Give your subscribers something worthy of their devotion, not just some disguised sales pitch, in return for giving you their undivided attention. This could be useful information, something free or discounted, or a special offer.

The trend I've been seeing is newsletters that are a *quick read*—brief and to the point. Publisher Joel Christopher of *Access-2-Success* e-zine has apparently latched onto this concept. Right after his opening remarks, he often includes a line such as, "Estimated Reading Time: 7.31 minutes." That way, readers know what to expect. I believe that the estimated reading time for newsletters and e-zines of the future will be well under five minutes.

GUIDELINES FOR WRITING ONLINE ADS, SIGNATURE FILES, AND BANNER COPY ▼

Writing online classified ads, e-zine and newsletter ads, signature files, banner copy, and other advertising copy for use on the web requires strategies a little different from offline ad writing. Where an offline ad might feature a strong benefit-laden headline, or give the product or service's unique selling proposition, writing your online ad requires a different kind of discipline—the same kind required to create an editorial as opposed to an advertisement. It's so easy to use short, punchy copy reminiscent of classified ads in the offline world, such as "Lose weight while you sleep. Click here to learn more," or "Learn a foreign language in 30 days. Click here for more information."

When you have only two to five lines in which to generate a response (such as in an online classified ad, advertising banner, or e-zine ad), it's tempting to resort to the tried-and-true techniques of advertising language. But do you really want your ad to say, "I'm an ad—read me?" No! On the Internet, you'll probably be ignored. The trick is to stand out above the other ads in the medium in which your ad is placed. This is accomplished not by screaming the loudest or using hype, exclamation points, capital letters, and so forth, but by featuring something *newsworthy* in your ad. Many editorial-style headlines could double as copy for online ads, with a bit of retooling, as necessary. For example:

> $2 Million Scientific Project Unlocks the Secret of Aging: How You Can Become Biologically Younger!" You can turn back your body's aging clock and be able to *prove it* with a simple at-home test. Read entire article here: http://www.domain.com.

You might think that getting someone to click on a link should be relatively easy. After all, clicking on a mouse seems like a virtually effortless task, doesn't it? It may appear so, but not when you consider that every commercial enterprise on the Internet is asking your prospects to do the same thing. The web population has learned to become selective about what they click on, particularly in view of the endless choices and the limited time at their disposal. You have to give them a compelling reason to click. Here is another example of an editorial-style ad.

> 9 Facts You Must Know Before You Buy Any Product That Promises to Grow Hair or Stop Hair Loss
>   Protect yourself from hair fallout and other horrors— and learn how to choose the right hair restoration product for your needs. Send a blank e-mail to 9facts@domain.com to receive free report.

The same applies to writing copy for banners, search engine listings, or SIG files.

Three Tips for Writing Online Ads

1) Make your ad look different, and articulate it differently from the rest of the ads in the medium where it runs so that yours will stand a chance at grabbing your audience's attention. Don't blend in with the rest.

2) Inject an element that will spark curiosity to get your audience to click.

3) Get prospects to opt-in, if possible, instead of trying to sell in the ad. In the offline world, this is called the two-step approach. Only amateurs and fools run three- to five-line classifieds and try to make a sale from that one ad. There's just not enough space in a few lines to make the sale. Use the ad as a lead generator to get people to opt in to receive a free report, a free course or a free eBook. That way, you acquire another qualified prospect to add to your mailing list.

Figure 6.2 is a SIG file I developed when I was working at Aesop Marketing Corporation. We ran it in both html and text versions. Both pulled a robust click-through rate.

After a few seconds, the html version (Figure 6.2) morphs into Figure 6.3, which simply has the wording.

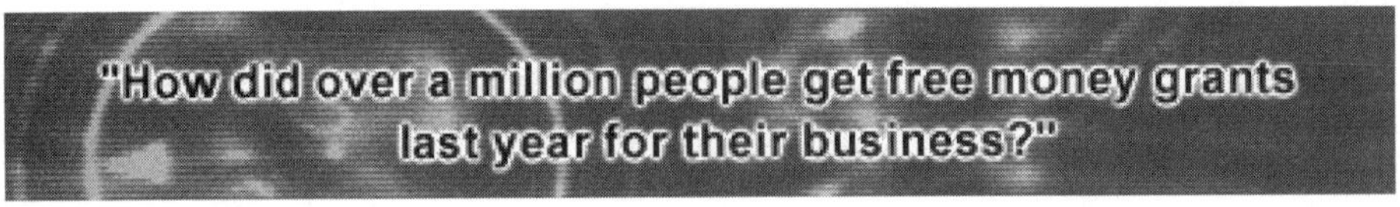

Figure 6.2

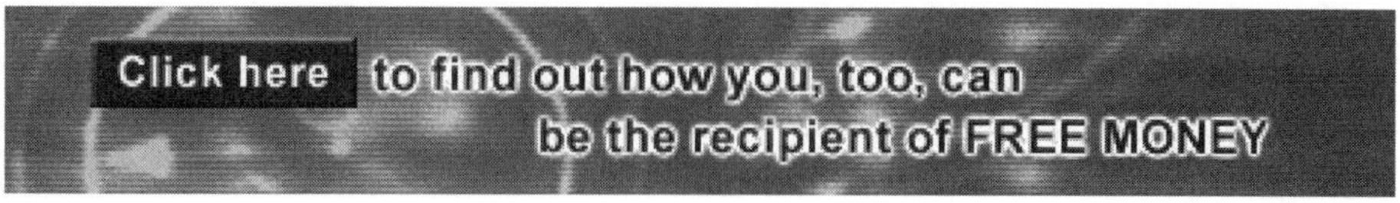

Click here to find out how you, too, can be the recipient of FREE MONEY

Figure 6.3

You may go to www.WebCopywritingUniversity.com/sig. htm to view the two-image signature file in action.

The text version reads as follows:

```
=====================
"How did over a million people get free money
grants last year for their businesses?" Click on
the link below to find out how you, too, can be the
recipient of free money.
http://www.freestuffforentrepreneursontheinternet.com
=====================
```

My own SIG file says simply:

```
Download your *free* eBook: "Frame-of-Mind Market-
ing: How to Convert Your Online Prospects into Cus-
tomers" at
http://www.webCopywritingUniversity.com/download.htm
```

The title of my e-book doubles as my sales pitch because it contains the entire benefit right there in the title. When people click on the link, they arrive at the download page, where I first collect their contact information and then allow them to start downloading. A captured name and e-mail address is more important than a site visit.

If you write an ad where readers must click on a link to go

to your webpage, they might choose to ignore it, and then you'll have nothing. On the other hand, if you offer to give readers something for free, if they do not visit your website you at least have their contact information. This is *gold* on the Internet because you can be in constant communication with them until they finally buy your product—and, more important, buy many other products from you.

Instead of directing readers to a download location as I did in my SIG file, you can opt to have them send a blank e-mail to your autoresponder to get the freebie. Either way, you will capture their e-mail address, because your web host sends you the e-mail address of everyone who sends a message to your autoresponder. The disadvantage here is that you don't get the person's first name—just an e-mail address—so you won't be able to personalize subsequent e-mails. However, the "send-a-blank-e-mail" method should not be discounted, because in online ads, SIG files, and bylines at the end of promotional articles, it is often easier to get people to send a blank e-mail to receive a freebie than to get them to click through to your website (where you can capture their first name and e-mail address via a form).

So much of your success depends on what you do *after* people visit your website. I estimate that up to 90 percent of your total sales will come from the skillful application of these follow-up marketing communications, combined with the e-mail strategies discussed in Chapter 5. Only a small number of visitors will become customers on their first visit to your website, but when you have mechanisms in place to capture the contact information of as many prospects as you can and start an e-mail relationship with them, that's when the real selling begins.

7

Last but Not Least:
Tying It All Together

Nothing in the world can take the place of persistence.
*Talent will not. Nothing is more common than unsuccessful
men with talent. Genius will not; unrewarded genius is
almost a proverb. Education will not; the world is full of
educated derelicts.* Persistence and determination alone
are omnipotent. *The slogan "Press on" has solved and
always will solve the problems of the human race.*
—Calvin Coolidge

Success in any endeavor, particularly in selling, is part ambition,
part observation, and part determination. Writing web copy that
sells is no different. As with any discipline, some people who
practice the principles discussed in this book will fail to meet

their sales objectives. Barring unrealistic expectations, I wish to offer solutions that will prevent that from happening. In this chapter we examine tracking and testing, troubleshoot web copy that is not generating sales, and present a four-step process to web copywriting success.

TRACK IT, FIX IT: WHAT TO DO WHEN WEB COPY IS *NOT* WORKING
▼

When I was creating offline copywriting, I learned one lesson I'll never forget. Do you remember those infomercials advertising contour pillows? In the original infomercials, the advertisers highlighted what they thought were the pillow's top two benefits: that they help you sleep better and make you more comfortable while you sleep.

When the pillows didn't sell too well, the advertisers phoned 100 actual buyers and asked them why they had purchased the pillows. Over half bought because of neck pain, the other half because of sleeplessness or because their spouse snored—benefits not even mentioned in the infomercial.

Based on these findings, they rewrote the pillow offer. Since 52 percent bought because of severe neck pain, the alleviation of neck pain became the lead benefit. Sales multiplied by more than ten times. Comfort Sleeper, the company that manufactures the pillows for Wal-Mart and the largest retail foam manufacturer in the United States, reported that sales in the stores went up 1,000 percent. The packaging for the entire industry changed to emphasize these benefits, and, as a result, a dormant product became a hot item overnight.

The advertiser also phoned people who didn't purchase (those who called the order line but decided not to order) or who returned the pillows. Those who did not purchase were confused by certain things said in the infomercial, and they had objections or questions that weren't answered to their satisfaction. Those who returned them said the pillows made their neck hurt more.

As a result, the ad company further refined the infomercial to remove the confusion and answer objections. Comfort Sleeper also put a note inside the package sent to pillow customers that forewarned them that their neck might hurt during the first few days of using the pillow because the neck was still adjusting to the contour, but that they could look forward to comfort after that (which was the truth). As a result, sales soared again, and, this time, returns were greatly reduced.

It all boils down to knowing your audience. Sometimes copywriters think they know their audience well, but, in actuality, they don't. In the case of the contour pillows, the ads overlooked key problems, pains, and predicaments (the three Ps) of the customers (neck pain, sleeplessness, and snoring spouses). Not until the phone survey provided feedback did the ad copy get it right.

Similarly, copywriters can guess what the target audience's hot buttons are, but if we don't know why people are buying the product or service, we won't know how to rewrite the copy if it isn't pulling in sales.

If you are the web copywriter hired to write the copy for a flat fee, you may not care much about this, except that you might not get repeat business. If, however, you're a web copywriter who is getting a percentage of the sales, or an Internet marketer who writes web copy for your own products and services, this will matter a great deal.

Surveying customers is so much simpler on the Internet. You no longer have to phone 100 people. All you need do is send a well-designed e-mail to those who bought the product and ask the following questions:

- ▶ "What are the reasons you bought this product or service, or what motivated you to buy?"

- ▶ "Can you list the top benefits of the product or service that convinced you to act?" Alternatively, you may prefer to list the main benefits and say, "Here are a few of the benefits of our product or service. Please rank them in order of importance."

When the copy I wrote for a diet pill website didn't pull as well as I expected, I used these questions in a minisurvey that I created for free at www.freeonlinesurveys.com, which then added a link in my e-mails to purchasers of the pills. All the customers had to do was click on the link and a pop-up appeared, which enabled them to answer and submit their answers in a matter of seconds. Therefore, I was able to do my research easily (and at zero cost) and make the necessary changes to the copy based on the survey findings.

For those who don't buy but have left their contact information and for those who return the product they bought, try asking the following questions:

Why didn't you buy?

What, if anything, was confusing about the offer?

Why did you return the product?

When you survey your customers, you often discover that the top benefit is something you buried somewhere in the middle of your web copy. Based on this information, you can restructure it accordingly. One of my clients, who sells a program that teaches people how to start their own promotional products (advertising specialties) business, used this headline on his website:

How to Get Your Share of the $18 Billion Promotional Products Industry

When it didn't pull, we surveyed those who bought the program and learned that the main reason they bought was because they wanted to find the factories that manufacture the promotional products. We rewrote the headline to read:

Start a lucrative promotional products profit center or distributorship easily with . . .

The Ultimate Resource for Finding Promotional Product Factory Sources

The new headline boosted response by 23 percent, without changing a single word of the body copy. We would not have had those incremental sales had we not bothered to query the customers. The bottom line is you must be willing to do what it takes to accomplish your objectives.

FOUR STEPS TO WEB COPYWRITING SUCCESS
▼

I learned a foolproof secret to success in any undertaking, and I've applied it to web copywriting, as follows:

Step 1. *Understand exactly what you want your web copy to accomplish.* In other words, define your objective, but this time, be more specific. If you can, quantify the results you want to get. It could be to convert 10 percent or more of your web visitors into customers, or to sell ten books per day, or to generate $1,000 in sales per day. Write down *exactly* what you want to accomplish.

Step 2. *Take action to fulfill your objective.* This includes writing the best possible web copy and marketing communications and getting traffic to your website (using linking strategies, search engine optimization, a revenue-sharing [affiliate] program, pay-per-click search engine advertising, or any other traffic-generating methods).

Step 3. *Observe what's working and what isn't working.* Track and test your results continually. Do more of what's working, and eliminate what's not working (including, but not limited to, key elements of your web copy).

Step 4. *Keep adjusting your actions.* Do this until you accomplish your desired objective.

When you do these four things, you'll never be without options. You'll never sit there and say, "Why does it work for others and not for me?" Probably the most important step is

Step 3, "Observe what's working and what isn't working." That is how I developed my own unique model of web copywriting, and I did it through tracking and testing.

On the Internet, you have to be tracking results and testing *continually*. I'm fortunate to have come from a web copywriting environment in which we tested everything. We tested e-mail subject lines; we tested whether personalizing the subject line was better than not personalizing the subject line. We tested lead-ins, dissonance elements, and various formats of newsletters. We tested web copy headlines, web designs, sites with pictures and those with no pictures. We even tested different prices, offers, guarantees, closes, and bullet points. You name it—we tested it.

However, as I mentioned earlier, things change so rapidly on the Internet that I cannot confidently say that what worked six months ago will still work as effectively today. Search engines change their algorithms constantly, spam filters and pop-up blockers are becoming ever vigilant, and acceptable business practices on the Internet are being altered by regulations and sanctions. That's why nothing beats the practice of constant testing and tracking to obtain your own marketing intelligence for your particular audience.

The kinds of things you discover when you track and test are astounding, and they affect the profitability of the website not just for the here and now, but also for the long term. Testing and tracking are so fundamental in direct-response marketing that they are a given; yet most people on the web don't test anything. They write the web copy once, they launch the product or service, and when it doesn't pull, they wonder why. They don't realize that tracking and testing can significantly boost the sales of a website.

While the concepts of tracking and testing would require another book to explain thoroughly, here are some fundamental concepts that will help you get started.

Track Your Results

We've discussed a number of marketing methods, including writing a free report or promotional article and disseminating it in newsletters and e-zines, ads in e-zines, online classified ads, pay-per-click advertising, a great SIG file that your affiliates use every time they send out e-mail, and so on. Let's assume that this month you did all of these things and you received a decent number of orders. What do you do next month? Repeat all of the same things again, right? *Wrong!*

You find out which things worked and which didn't so that you can repeat more of what worked and none of what didn't. If, for instance, you determine that your free report that ran in an e-zine last month accounted for 93 percent of your sales, and the online classified ads did not produce a single sale, then you would contact more e-zine and newsletter publishers to run your free report, and you'd cancel your online classified ads.

You may have heard of John Wanamaker, the famous merchant who helped usher in the age of the department store in the early twentieth century. John Wanamaker was reputed to have said, "I know that half of the money I spend on advertising is wasted; but I can never find out which half." That doesn't have to be your problem, since there are so many ways you can track sales made on the Internet.

The thing to remember is that it isn't *you* who decides what works, no matter how many years of experience you have in marketing, nor is it you who determines the best-performing headline, offer, guarantee, or price. Nothing works until the tests prove it works.

Marketing great Ted Nicholas, who reportedly spent over $500,000 testing and tracking copy elements, asserts that simply by changing the headline, you can increase the pulling power of a direct-response ad by 1,700 percent, even when the rest of the ad is identical! The only way to learn this is through testing.

Let's say you are running an ad that's pulling a 2 percent click-to-sale conversion rate. You figure since 2 percent is a decent response rate, you're earning a net profit of $1,000, and your advertising cost is $500, you can't complain. Why, that's a 100 percent return on my investment, you say to yourself. But what if you discover, through testing, that another one of your ads pulls a 4 percent response rate, you're earning a net profit of $2,000, and, since your advertising is a fixed cost of $500, that means you increased the return on your investment from $500 to $1,500, or from 100 percent to 400 percent!

Online, many programs and scripts are available that enable you to test and track results. For instance, *rotator scripts* allow you to track the clicks and sales generated by two or more different versions of copy.

Ad tracking software or services allow you to test and track results without hassles. In a nutshell, here's how these services work: A redirection URL is assigned to each campaign you run, which allows you to count actions such as clicks, sales, and sign-ups to your newsletter or opt-in offer. It allows you to view detailed information and analysis for each campaign: for example, how your pay-per-click campaign is doing at Overture (a search engine), how your ad in the Yahoo! classifieds is doing, how that free report that you're giving away via autoresponder is doing, and so on and so forth.

In addition to these basic tracking functions, a tracking service allows you to evaluate all your visitors' click trails so that you can:

1. Know exactly what trail buyers take and, as a result, streamline your site to get all visitors to follow that proven linear path

2. See what paths nonbuyers take and eliminate the bottlenecks and roadblocks at your site

3. See what visitors who subscribe to your newsletter or opt into your lead-generation system really do on your site

4. See which traffic sources create the most sales—or no sales—so you know where to focus your efforts

For those of you who have newsletters or e-zines or who run e-mail marketing campaigns, there are also good direct e-mail marketing services that enable you to easily track and test the results of your e-mail marketing. For example, you can find out who opened your e-mail message, who clicked on which link, what they looked at on your website, how long they stayed on your site, whether they bought something, which item(s) they bought, how much they spent, and who they are, based on demographic and registration data.

Here are four e-mail services that track and test results:

www.emaillabs.com

www.email-marketing-central.com

www.gotmarketing.com

www.constantcontact.com

TRAFFIC GENERATION: GETTING THE WORD OUT AND THE VISITORS IN ▼

A website with killer copy but no traffic is like a beautiful store filled with desirable merchandise located in the boondocks—people will never find it. What good are killer copy, opt-in offers, autoresponders that convert website visitors into customers, and all the tracking devices in the world if no one stops by to visit?

Throughout this book, we've focused on the traffic-conversion part of the Internet marketing equation, but we can't leave the subject without touching briefly on the traffic-generation part of the equation.

The topic of traffic generation is vast, and it would require another volume to do it justice. Therefore, I've limited my discussion to a few strategies that have been effective in my own experience.

Search Engine Positioning

Whenever the subject of traffic generation is discussed, invariably search engine positioning comes up. Some Internet experts contend that an estimated 86 percent of the average website's traffic comes from search engines. While it is true that website promotions that include search engine positioning and optimization may contribute to a website's success, a website can nevertheless succeed without it, as long as it employs other traffic-generation strategies. I've seen highly profitable websites that get little or no search engine exposure. Still, no discussion of traffic generation would be complete without the topic of search engine positioning.

I've spent almost eight years in Internet marketing, and I've learned that trying to get top search engine rankings is a major undertaking that is best left in the hands of professional search engine positioning and optimization experts. Seeking high search engine rankings in all the major search engines is a complex undertaking that requires diligence and attention because the search engines use different algorithms (sets of rules) to rank pages. Even if you succeed in satisfying all the algorithms, those algorithms change constantly, which means if you get the advice that tells you to have your target keyword appear no more than 12 times on your home page, that advice is probably obsolete by the time you hear it. The search engines are always five steps ahead of everyone.

For this reason, I leave search engine positioning to professionals who specialize in that field. Trying to maintain a high search engine ranking is a time-consuming endeavor, and requires constant maintenance, so I do what I'm good at and let search engine professionals do what they're good at.

The Internet abounds with search engine professionals who can guarantee that your website listing will appear in the top 10, top 20, or top 30 search results in the major search engines under specific keywords or phrases. Do a search on any search engine for the keywords, "search engine optimization" or "search engine ranking" and you'll find hundreds, if not thousands of professionals who can improve the ranking of your website, thereby increasing your website traffic.

Pay-per-Click Search Engines

Pay-per-click search engines are search engines that allow you to pay for placement or ranking in their particular search engine. This is an effective way to attract inexpensive, targeted traffic to your website because you pay only for eyeballs of people who actually click through to your website. Overture is the leader of the pack when it comes to pay-per-click search engines. The minimum bid is 5 cents per click, but in order to have your listing among the top search results, the per-click price you would need to bid may have to be considerably higher, depending on the popularity of your keywords or how highly searched or how competitive your keywords are.

Here's an example of how pay-per-click economics work: If you bid 50 cents per click for the keywords "water purifier," and 100 people click through to your website, your cost would be $50 (100 clicks × 50 cents). If you happen to be bidding for highly competitive words, it may cost you $2.00 or more per click, but that's because many more people search for those words, which drives up the bid price.

In the end though, it doesn't matter how high you bid or whether you're ranked number one in the search results, because if your listing is not compelling, no one will click. Overture allows you to create your own listing, so when you design your listing, make sure you follow the guidelines for writing online ads while at the same time abiding by the rules of Overture (or any other pay-per-click search engine). With a well-constructed listing, you can at least be assured that you will get a good percentage of click-throughs to your website.

Caveat emptor: Do not—I repeat, *do not*—bid to have a high ranking if you do not have killer copy on your website backing you up. All the clicks in the world are worth nothing if your web copy doesn't convert those visitors into customers.

Overture is the top pay-per-click search engine, followed in popularity by FindWhat.com. There are several hundred pay-per-click search engines out there, and if you want to know who they are, as well as to get tips and strategies about using pay-per-click search engines, go to www.payperclicksearchengines.com/.

Linking Strategies

Another way to get top rankings in the search engines—without really trying—is by getting other websites to link to your website. The algorithms of the search engines take the number of websites linking to your website into consideration when ranking you. The more websites that link to you, the higher your search engine ranking.

One of the top Internet marketing websites is Ralph Wilson's website at www.Wilsonweb.com, a site that consistently ranks very high on the search engines under highly searched and extremely competitive keywords like "web marketing" and "e-commerce." Ralph Wilson is one of my business acquaintances, so a couple of years ago, I asked him how he achieved such high search engine rankings. He said he just provides solid, bona fide content and gets other websites to link to his website. Last time I checked, Wilsonweb.com had 2,946 websites linked to it. It's no wonder, then, that search engines rank Wilsonweb.com high in their search results.

The more websites linking to your website, the higher your search engine ranking. Even more important, when you get those websites to link to your site, your website will be exposed to all the web visitors of all those websites that link to you, and that means more web traffic and more sales. The key is to get websites with high traffic to link to you. If you get dozens of high-traffic websites funneling their traffic to yours, you'll be amazed how much traffic you can get. Once you get a link from a website, the link will probably stay up forever, paying you dividends in terms of traffic for weeks, months, and years to come.

Of course, websites won't be inclined to link to your site if all you have on your site is copy that reeks of advertising, which is yet another reason to aim for an editorial style of writing crafted with hidden selling.

How to Get Websites to Link to Your Site. There's a long, tedious way of doing it, and there's an easy, painless way. I'll tell you about the long, tedious way first so that you'll really appreciate the easy, painless way that I will show you.

The long, tedious way is to scour the web looking for websites that are most likely to link to yours. You'd use a search engine and type in a keyword or phrase that would yield websites that are similar to or related to your website. For example, if you have a website that sells widgets, you'd search for websites catering to widget users, the widget industry, and so on.

When you get your search results, you'll have to scroll through the hundreds, even thousands, of websites and click through to them one by one to find the contact information or the e-mail address of someone to whom you can send your linking proposal. Then you have to type an e-mail to every e-mail address you find, cross your fingers, and hope that after spending countless hours doing this, some of them will say yes, they'll link to your site.

The easy and painless way is to use two invaluable tools that you can download for free. The first is webFerret, at www.ferretsoft.com, and the second is 2bpop, at www.2bpop.com/. They work beautifully in tandem. Once you've downloaded them, go to one of your website's competitors—one that has many websites linking to it. Using webFerret, you can then pull up every single site on the Internet that links to your competitor's site and save the list. Next, open 2bpop, which will automatically find an e-mail address on that website; 2bpop allows you to load and send the same template e-mail very rapidly. You can even set it up so that your 2bpop merges information from the website you're viewing into your template e-mail. This makes the process lightning fast.

E-Zines and Newsletters

If you've been involved in Internet marketing for any length of time, you've probably heard it said that dollar for dollar, the best marketing promotion you can do is to run ads in other people's e-zines and newsletters with the same target audience as yours. Even better is to write compelling promotional articles or free reports and offer them as content to websites, newsletters, and e-zines. We've already discussed how to write these articles and reports.

Type the keywords "directory of e-zines" or "e-zine directory" on any search engine and you'll find resources that list e-zines and online publications in which you can advertise or submit content.

It hasn't escaped anyone's attention that the Internet has become a global marketplace such as the world has never known. Fortunes have been made, and will continue to be made. In this book, I've set forth copywriting principles that work in both online and offline markets, and I've pointed out important distinctions required of web copy. While human nature remains constant, consumers' buying habits are different on the web than they are when presented with information from other media such as direct mail, TV, or radio. Communication has a different texture online, and those who can discern and appreciate the nuances between communicating online and offline are destined to profit the most from Internet selling.

Although the World Wide Web is a medium where practically anyone who has anything to sell can market every day at little or no cost, there are unwritten rules that online businesses must follow. The challenge to marketers, if they are to have long-term marketing success on the web, is to abide by the rules while using creative approaches that operate well within those parameters.

The information presented here should act as a springboard for further discussion and as a tool for helping website owners and web copywriters make decisions. Although the principles have been validated through extensive research and testing, research is nothing but a tool, not an absolute truth. There are no absolute truths in a rapidly changing cyberworld that is in a constant state of flux. Selling on the web is a growing art that will undoubtedly reinvent itself many times over in our lifetimes.

That said, my aim has been to take the guesswork out of direct-response online selling and to give you a running start on your own web copywriting adventure.

Index